PROBABILITY METHODS

NCEA Level 2 External

Charlotte Walker and Victoria Walker

Walker Maths 2.12 Probability
1st Edition
Charlotte Walker
Victoria Walker

Editor: Eva Chan
Cover and text design: Cheryl Smith, Macarn Design
Production controller: Siew Han Ong
Reprint: Jess Lovell

Any URLs contained in this publication were checked for currency during the production process. Note, however, that the publisher cannot vouch for the ongoing currency of URLs.

Acknowledgements
Cover photo courtesy of Shutterstock.
We wish to thank the Boards of Trustees of Darfield and Riccarton High Schools for allowing us to use materials and ideas developed while teaching. Our thanks also go to all past and present colleagues who have generously shared their expertise and ideas.

For product information and technology assistance,
in Australia call **1300 790 853**;
in New Zealand call **0800 449 725**

For permission to use material from this text or product, please email **aust.permissions@cengage.com**

National Library of New Zealand Cataloguing-in-Publication Data
A catalogue record for this book is available from the National Library of New Zealand.

ISBN 978 017 0 354240

Cengage Learning Australia
Level 7, 80 Dorcas Street
South Melbourne, Victoria Australia 3205

Cengage Learning New Zealand
Unit 4B Rosedale Office Park
331 Rosedale Road, Albany, North Shore 0632, NZ

For learning solutions, visit **cengage.co.nz**

Printed in China by 1010 Printing International Limited
25 25

CONTENTS

ISBN: 9780170354240

Formula

This is the formula for this achievement standard.

Standard normal distribution	$Z = \frac{x - \mu}{\sigma}$

Glossary

Make your own glossary of key terms:

Term	Definition	Picture/Example
Mode		
Frequency		
Proportion		
Probability		
Percentage		

ISBN: 9780170354240

P(A′)		
Continuous data		
Discrete data		
Parameters		
Mean (μ or $\bar{x}$)		
Standard deviation (σ or s)		
Normal distribution		
Standard normal distribution		
Absolute risk		
Relative risk		
Either		

ISBN: 9780170354240

Probability revision

Range of values that probability can take:

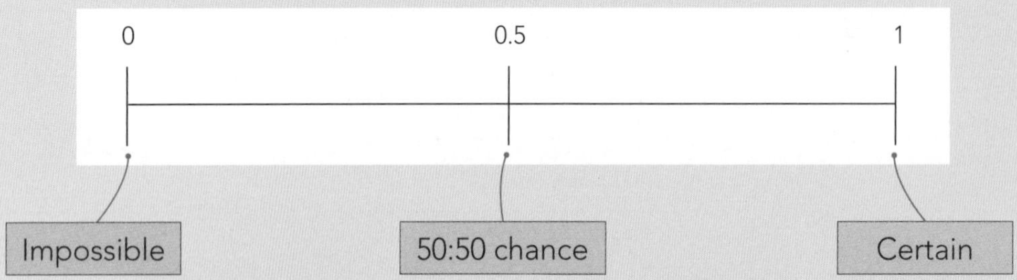

Ways of calculating probabilities:

1 Equally likely outcomes: Probability = $\dfrac{\text{number of favourable outcomes}}{\text{total possible outcomes}}$

Example: for a fair die, P(5 or 6) = $\dfrac{2}{6}$

2 Long run relative frequency: Probability = $\dfrac{\text{number of times an event occurs}}{\text{total number of trials}}$

Example:
P(Anna is late to school) = $\dfrac{\text{number of times she has been late to school in the last year}}{\text{total number of school days in the last year}}$

Expected number of outcomes = P(event) x number of trials

Example: If P(Anna is late to school) = 0.04, and there are 50 days in the term, then:

expected number of late arrivals by Anna in the term = 0.04 x 50 = 2

Combining probabilities:

and ⟶ x
or ⟶ +

Examples:

1 If you flip a coin and then toss a die, the probability of getting a head **and** then a 2
$= \dfrac{1}{2} \times \dfrac{1}{6} = \dfrac{1}{12}$

2 If you toss a fair die once, the probability of getting an even number **or** a 1
$= \dfrac{1}{2} + \dfrac{1}{6} = \dfrac{4}{6} = \dfrac{2}{3}$

ISBN: 9780170354240

Test yourself

For the following situations, indicate whether each is right or wrong, and justify your decision.

✔ ✖

1 Mike calculated that the probability of winning his game was 1.05.

Justification:

2 Miranda wrote down that the probability of getting an even number when a die was tossed is 0.5. The answer said it was $\frac{1}{2}$ so she marked it wrong.

Justification:

3 Twenty-five members of Archie's class own a pet. If there are 28 in the class, the probability that a class member owns a cat = $\frac{28}{25}$.

Justification:

4 At Archie's school, a quarter of the students travel to school on a bus. Therefore Archie expects that seven students from his class will catch a bus to school.

Justification:

5 Juliet has a 10-sided die with the numbers 1 to 10 written on the faces. If she tosses it once, the probability of getting an odd number or a 10 = $\frac{1}{20}$.

Justification:

6 Using the same die, the probability that he gets two 10s when he tosses it twice = 0.01.

Justification:

7 Angus calculates that the probability it will rain tomorrow is -0.01.

Justification:

8 A fair six-sided die is tossed once. The probability of getting a 2 or a 3 = $\frac{1}{3}$.

Justification:

ISBN: 9780170354240

Graphs of distributions

Calculations from graphs of distributions

The graph below shows test scores for 50 students.

'Frequency' is the number of students getting each score.

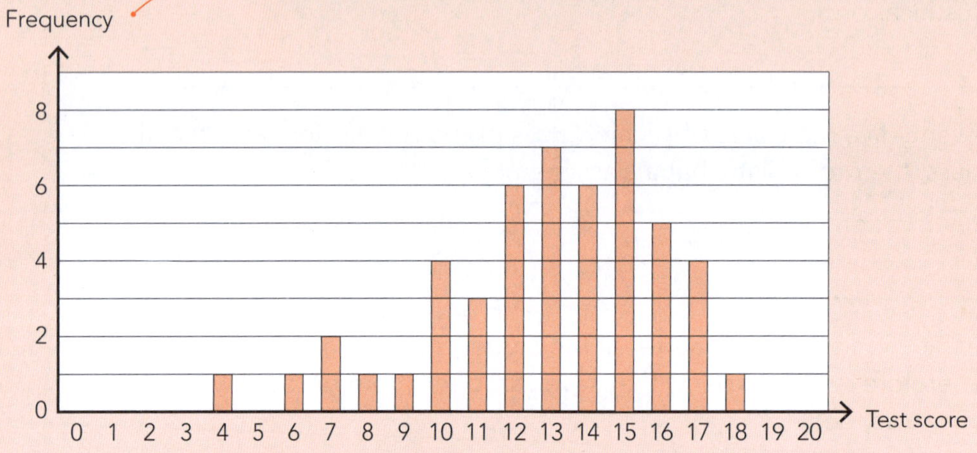

Frequency

8
6
4
2
0

0 1 2 3 4 5 6 7 8 9 10 11 12 13 14 15 16 17 18 19 20 Test score

a How many students earned 12 marks?

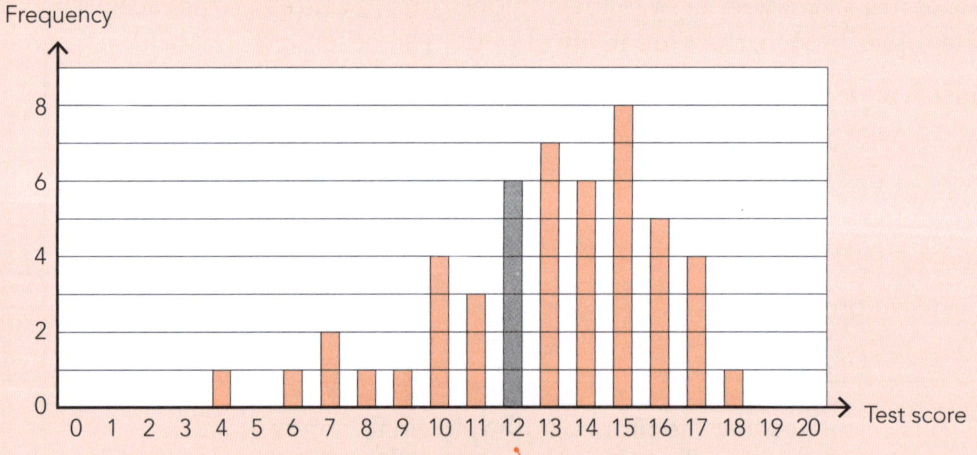

Frequency

8
6
4
2
0

0 1 2 3 4 5 6 7 8 9 10 11 12 13 14 15 16 17 18 19 20 Test score

Because the column above 12 goes up to 6, we know that 6 students got 12 marks.

ISBN: 9780170354240

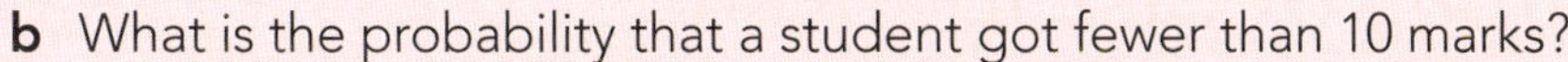

b What is the probability that a student got fewer than 10 marks?

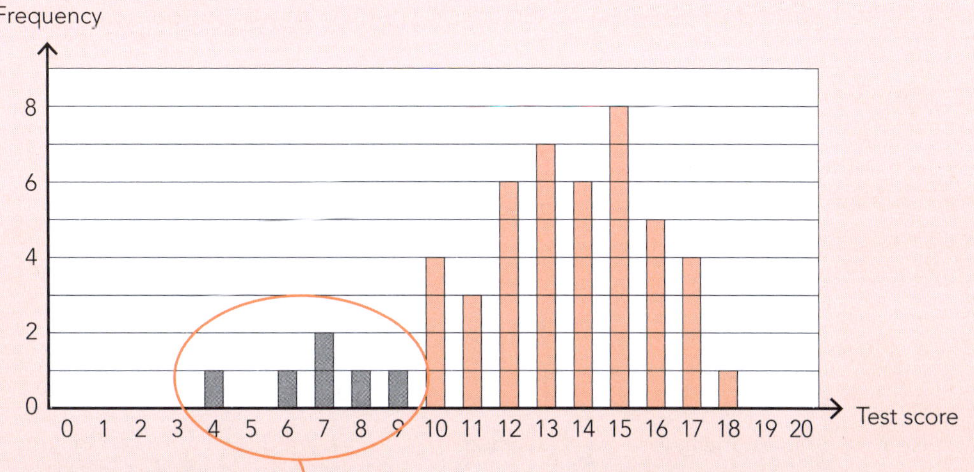

Because there are 6 students in the columns to the left of 10, and there were 50 students in total, the probability that a student got fewer than 10 is $\frac{6}{50} = 0.12$.

c What percentage of students got marks that were fewer than 10 or more than 16?

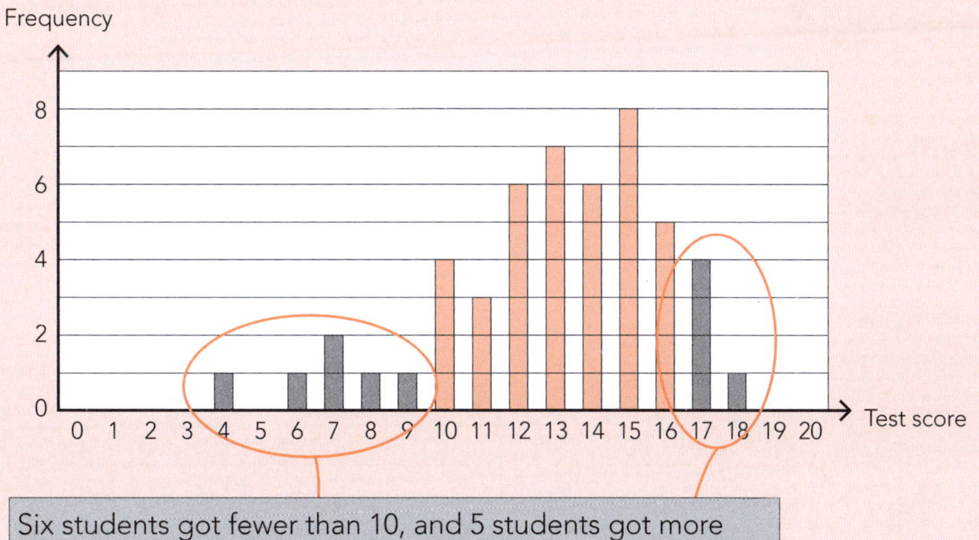

Six students got fewer than 10, and 5 students got more than 16. This totals 11 out of 50 students, or 22%.

ISBN: 9780170354240

Describing graphs of distributions

Features to state and discuss when describing or comparing distributions:

1 The lowest and highest values: these indicate where on the x-axis the distribution is located.
2 The range (highest value – lowest value): this indicates the width of the distribution.
3 The mode(s): these indicate(s) the highest point(s) of the distribution.
4 The shape:

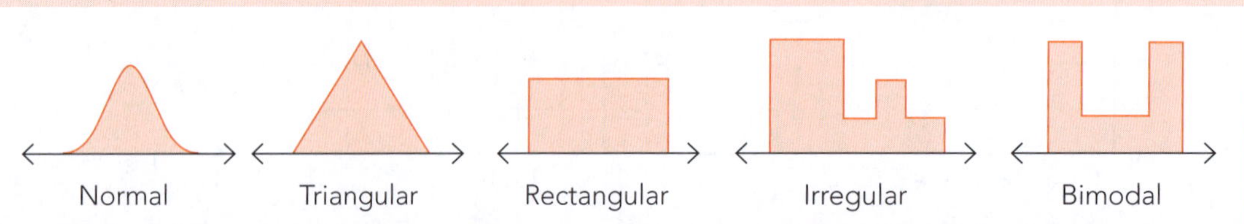

5 Symmetry: the graph may be symmetrical:

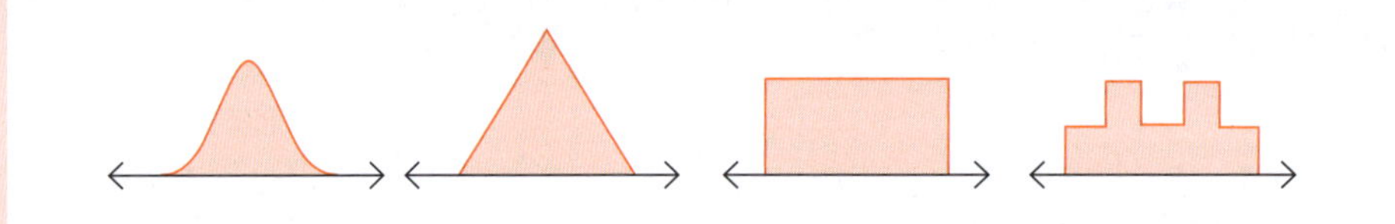

Or asymmetrical:

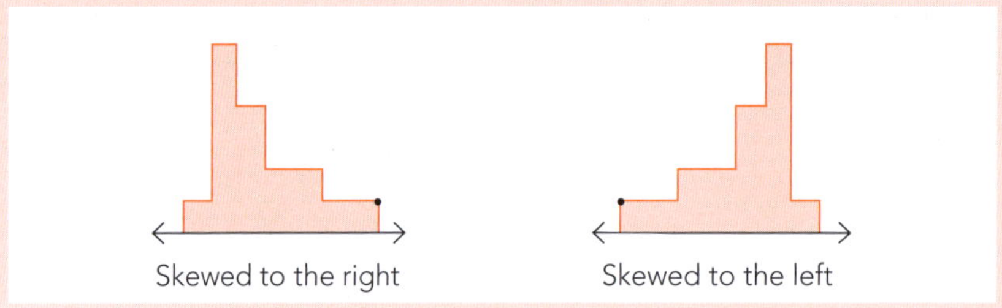

Example:

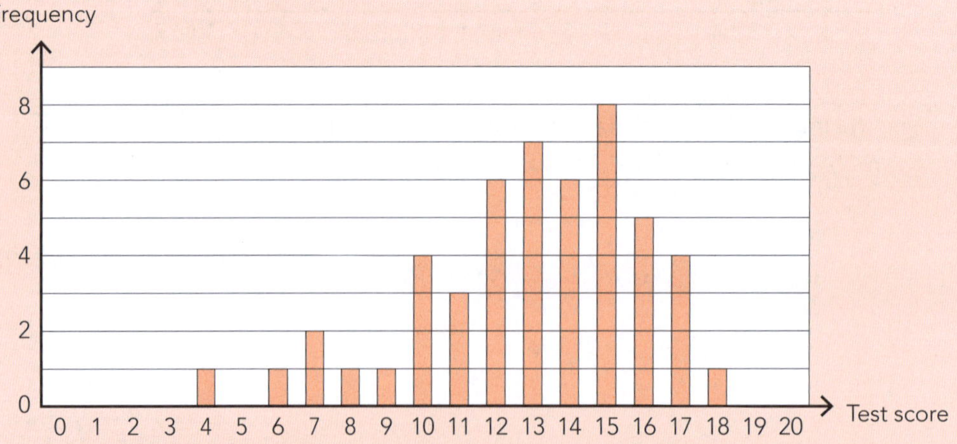

The values in this graph are all between 4 and 18, with a range of 14. The mode is 15. The shape is almost triangular, and asymmetrical as it is skewed to the left.

ISBN: 9780170354240

Look at the following graphs and answer the questions.

1 Jemimah set up a simulation on her computer so that 100 playing cards were drawn one by one from a 52-card pack, and then replaced. The graph of the distribution is shown below.

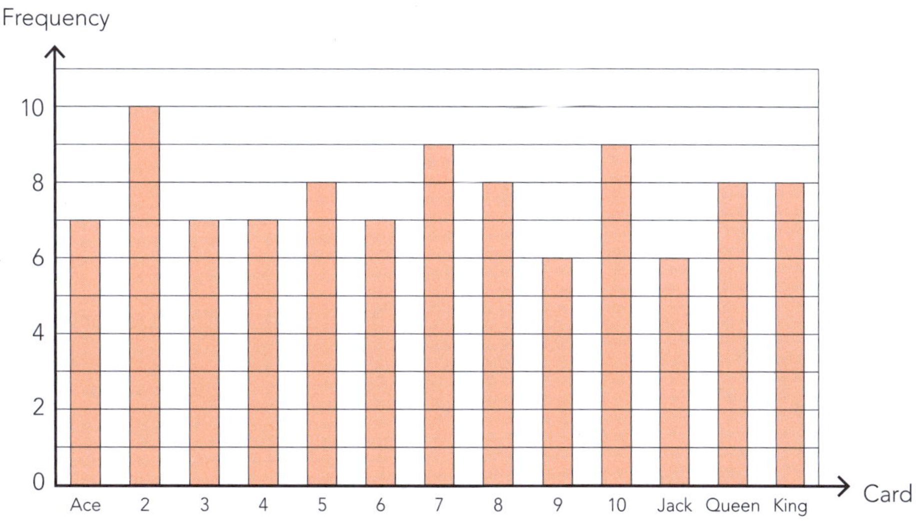

a Based on this simulation, calculate the probability of a picture card (Jack, Queen or King) being drawn.

b Compare this with the theoretical probability that a picture card is drawn from a real 52-card pack of cards. Why are these values different?

c Based on the simulation, calculate the probability of drawing a 6 or a 9.

d Describe this distribution.

e Jemimah reset her computer to repeat this, but she draws 1000 cards. How would you expect this second distribution to differ from her first one?

ISBN: 9780170354240

2 Happy Hire bought 60 new cars in 2014. The number of faults in these vehicles during their first year is shown below.

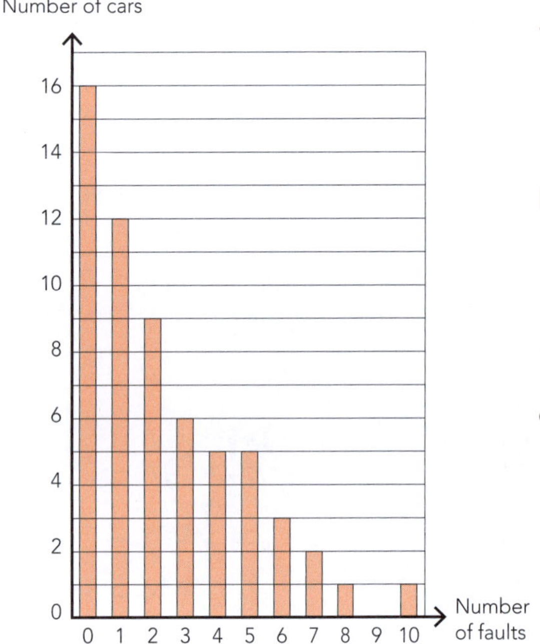

a What percentage of cars had no faults?

b What proportion of cars had more than two faults?

c Describe this distribution.

3 Rogue Rentals buys 69 vehicles of a different type. The number of faults in these vehicles during their first year is shown below.

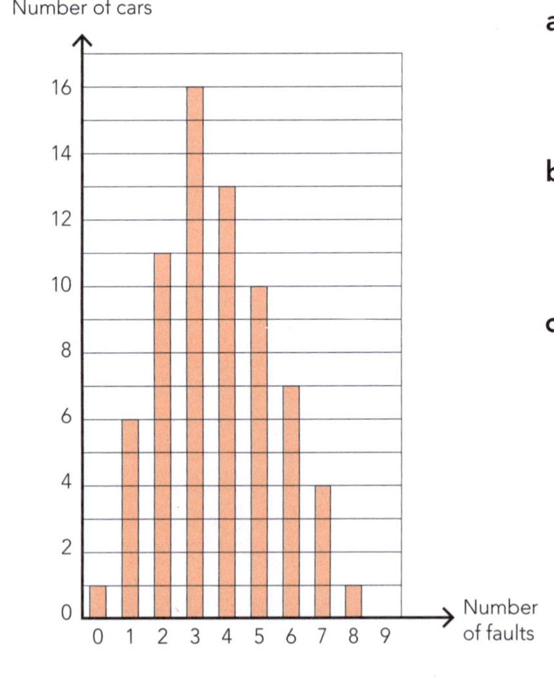

a What percentage of cars had no faults?

b What was the most common number of faults in a car?

c Write a paragraph comparing the distributions of faults for the two companies.

ISBN: 9780170354240

4 The heights of a group of 40 Year 7 students are shown on the graph below.

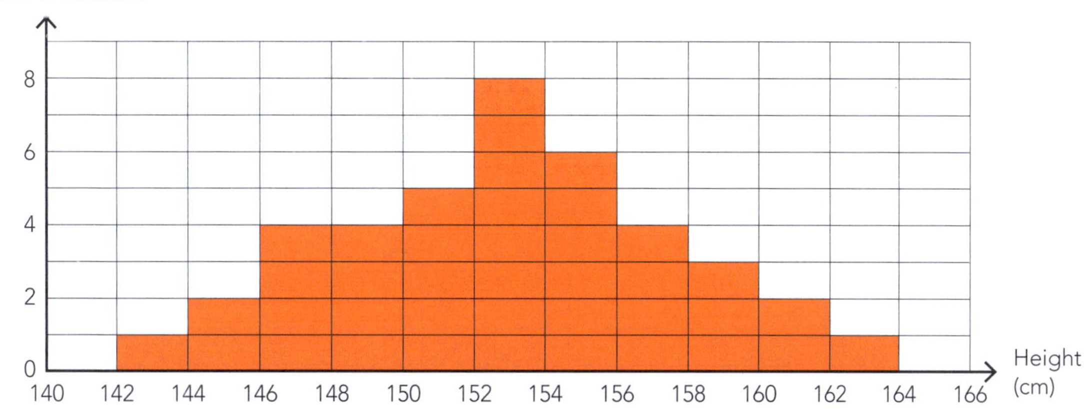

a What proportion of the students was over 158 cm?

b What is the probability that a student in this group is between 150 cm and 160 cm?

c Describe this graph.

The following graph shows the heights of 40 students from Year 8 at the same school.

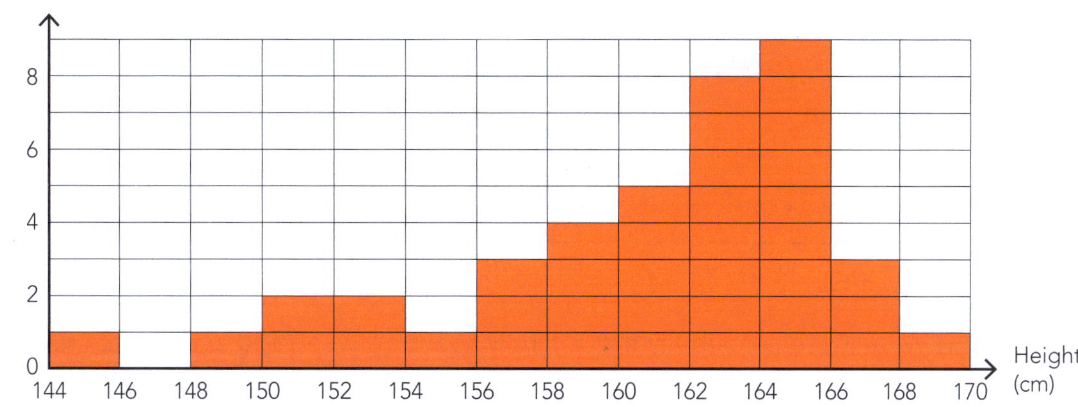

d Compare the proportions of students who were over 158 cm in the two groups.

ISBN: 9780170354240

5 The graph shows the weights of 65 takahe in a population on an offshore island.

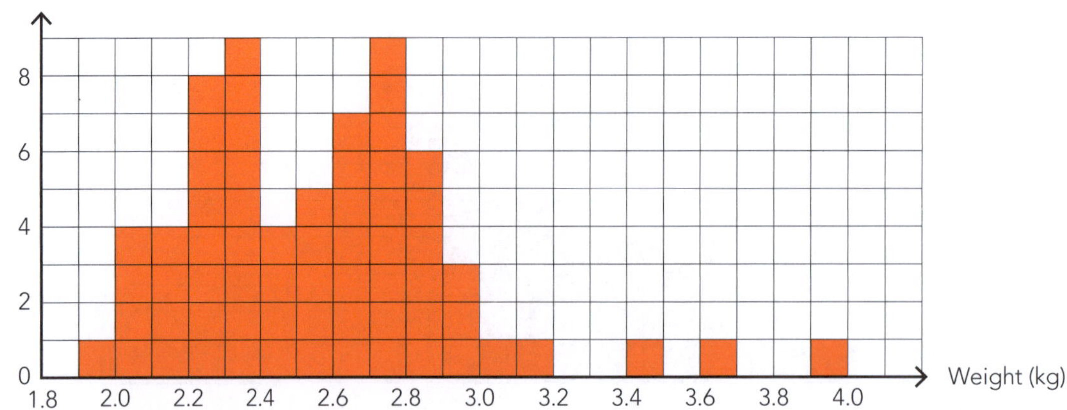

a What percentage of these birds was over 3 kg?

____

b What is the probability that a bird is between 2.5 kg and 3.0 kg?

____

c Describe this distribution.

____

____

6 The graph shows the amount spent by 40 families at an A&P Show.

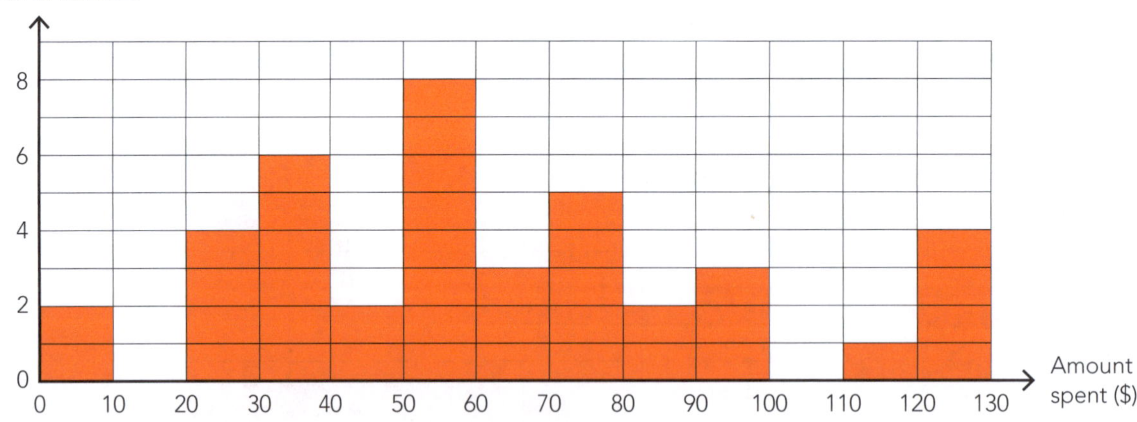

a What is the probability that a family spent between $50 and $70 at this show?

____

____

b Describe the distribution.

____

____

ISBN: 9780170354240

7 An analysis of the number of pages in a sample of 76 New Zealand novels published in the last five years produces the following results:

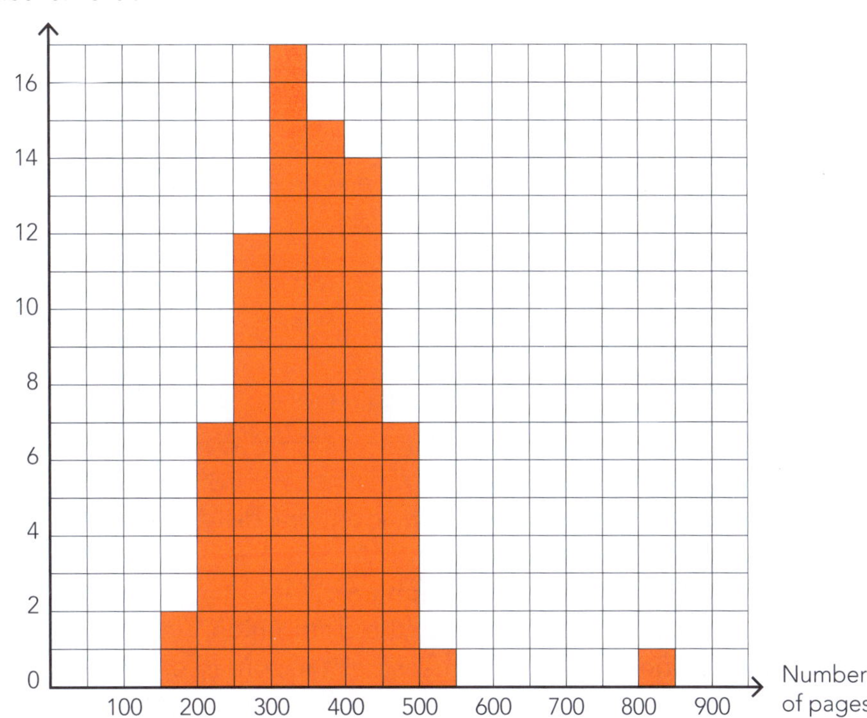

a Write a paragraph describing the distribution.

____

____

____

____

____

b Calculate the percentage of novels that have fewer than 250 pages.

____

____

c Between what values does the mode lie?

____

____

ISBN: 9780170354240

The normal distribution

This is used when:

- We have **measured** (continuous) data, for example heights, distances, mass, area.
- Most data is clustered around a central value, with a few extreme values either side.
- The distribution is symmetrical.

The general shape:

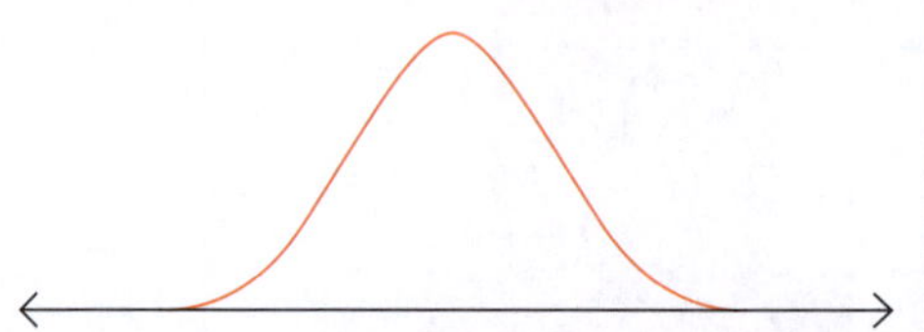

Parameters are the things we need to know about any distribution.

The parameters for the normal distribution are:

- the **mean** (μ or $\bar{x}$): this is at the centre of the distribution.
- the **standard deviation** (σ or s): this measures the spread of the distribution, and occurs at the point of inflection in the curve. Nearly all values lie within three standard deviations of the mean.

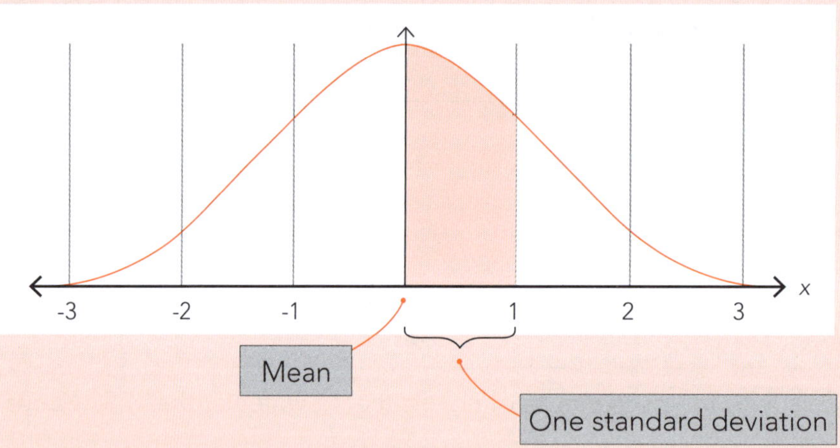

However, normal distribution curves vary widely, depending on their means and standard deviations.

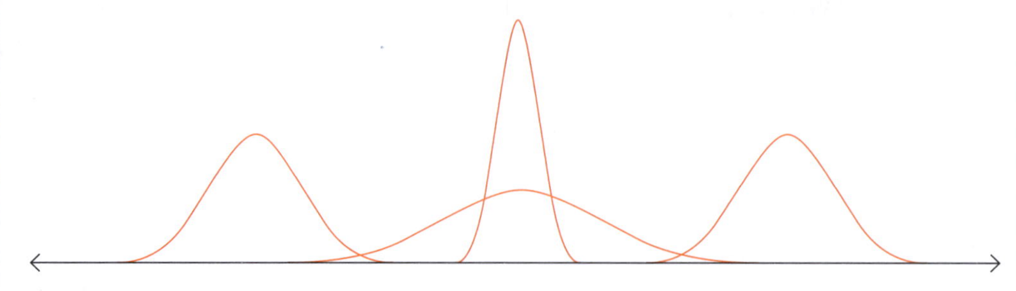

Consequently we need a **standard normal distribution**.

ISBN: 9780170354240

The standard normal distribution

The probability of an event lying between two values is represented by the **area** under the curve. Calculating this is very complicated, so we have tables of probabilities that can be looked up. Because we can't have a set of tables for every different distribution, we convert individual normal distributions to the **standard normal distribution**.

The **parameter** for the **standard normal distribution** is **Z**: For any value of x, Z measures the number of standard deviations to the right or left of the mean.

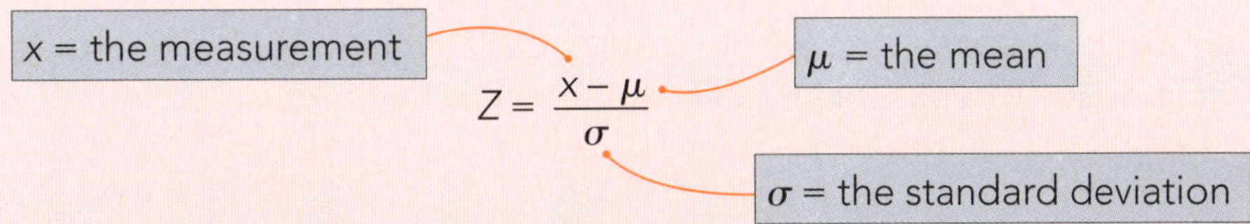

Example: Consider a distribution of heights, with a mean of 150 cm and a standard deviation of 5 cm.

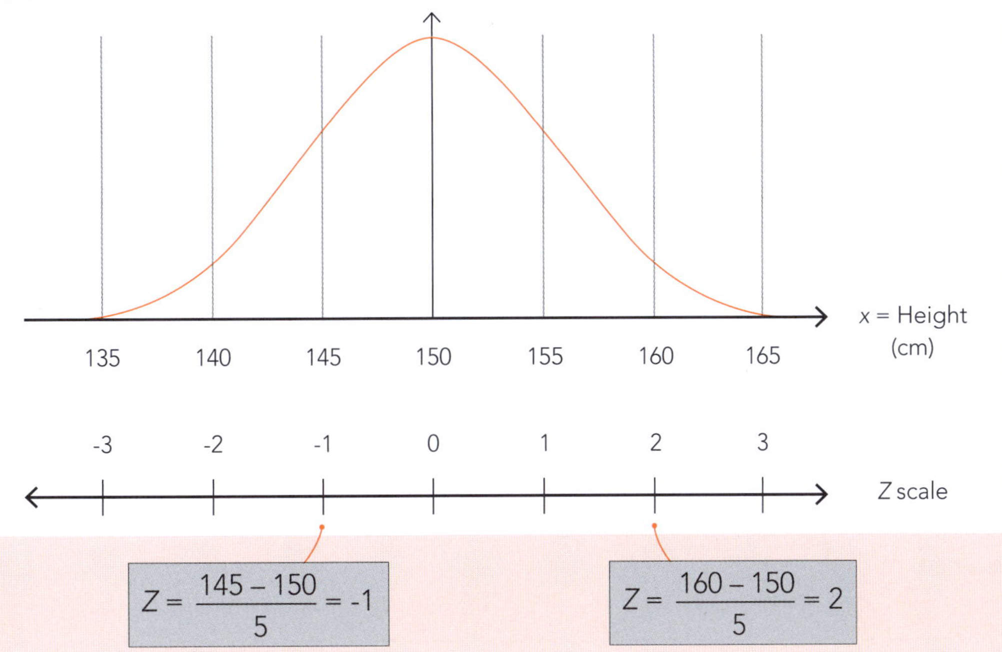

$$Z = \frac{145 - 150}{5} = -1$$

$$Z = \frac{160 - 150}{5} = 2$$

Example: The volume of milk in bottles has a mean of 1005 mL with a standard deviation of 2 mL.
Calculate the Z values for:

1008 mL: $Z = \frac{x - \mu}{\sigma} = \frac{1008 - 1005}{2} = 1.5$

1000 mL: $Z = \frac{x - \mu}{\sigma} = \frac{1000 - 1005}{2} = -2.5$

ISBN: 9780170354240

Calculate the value of Z for each of the following situations.

1 The weights of bars of soap have a mean of 102 g, with a standard deviation of 1.5 g. Calculate Z values for bars which weigh:

a 105 g

---

b 100 g

---

2 The lengths of liquorice straps have a mean of 355 mm, with a standard deviation of 2 mm. Calculate Z values for straps with the following lengths:

a 355 mm

---

b 360 mm

---

c 349 mm

---

3 The areas of sections in a subdivision have a mean of 560 m^2, with a standard deviation of 22 m^2. Calculate Z values for sections with the following areas:

a 605 m^2

---

b 470 m^2

---

4 The average lung capacity of teenagers is 4.8 L, with a standard deviation of 0.35 L. Calculate Z values for teenagers with the following lung capacities:

a 4.7 L

---

b 5.7 L

---

5 The track lengths on a CD have a mean of 3 minutes and 18 seconds, with a standard deviation of 11 seconds. Calculate Z values for tracks of the following lengths (convert these times to seconds first):

a 2 minutes and 23 seconds

---

b 3 minutes and 52 seconds

ISBN: 9780170354240

1 Calculating probabilities

Using Z to calculate a probability

Remember the range of possible values for probabilities:

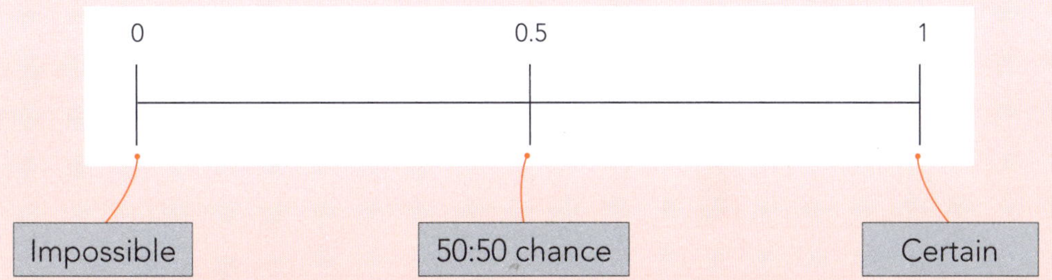

- If something is **certain** to occur, its probability is 1.
- We know that the area under a normal distribution curve represents probabilities of everything that can occur, so that area must be 1.
- The normal curve is **symmetrical**, so the area under each half must be 0.5.

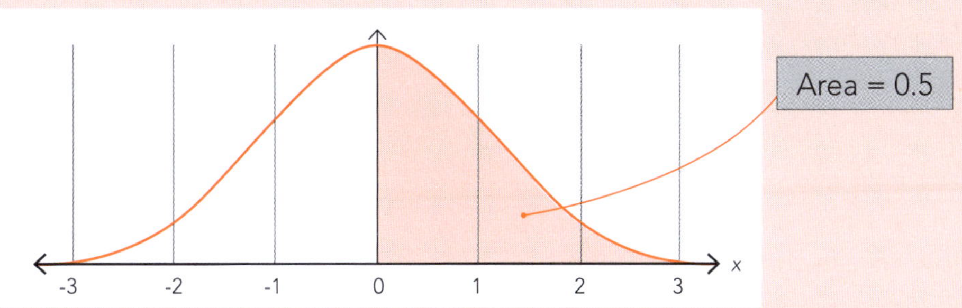

- From the tables we also know these values:

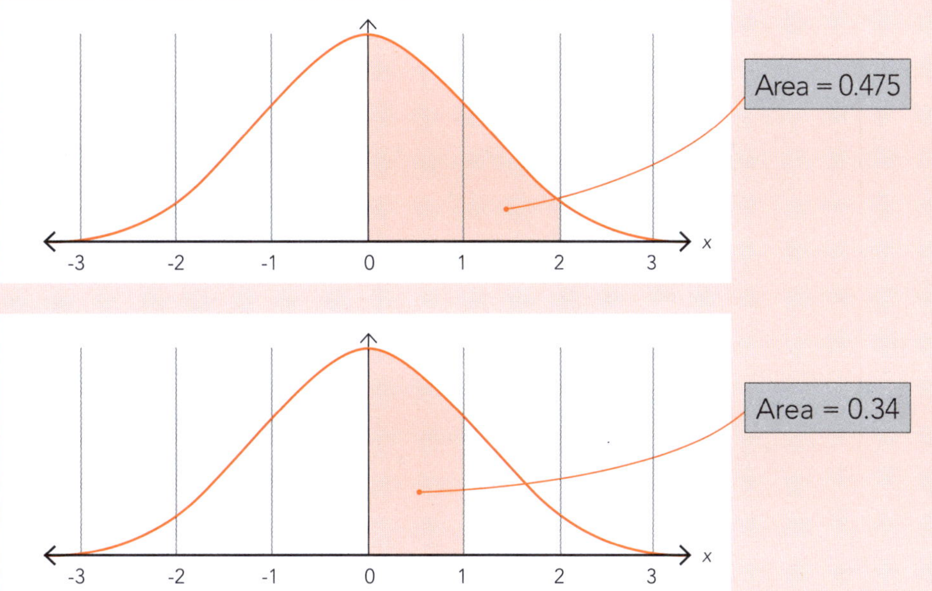

- Tables and graphics calculators can give us probabilities for **any** values of Z.
- Because the graph is **symmetrical**, we can use these to calculate any probabilities under a normal distribution curve.

ISBN: 9780170354240

Reading normal distribution tables

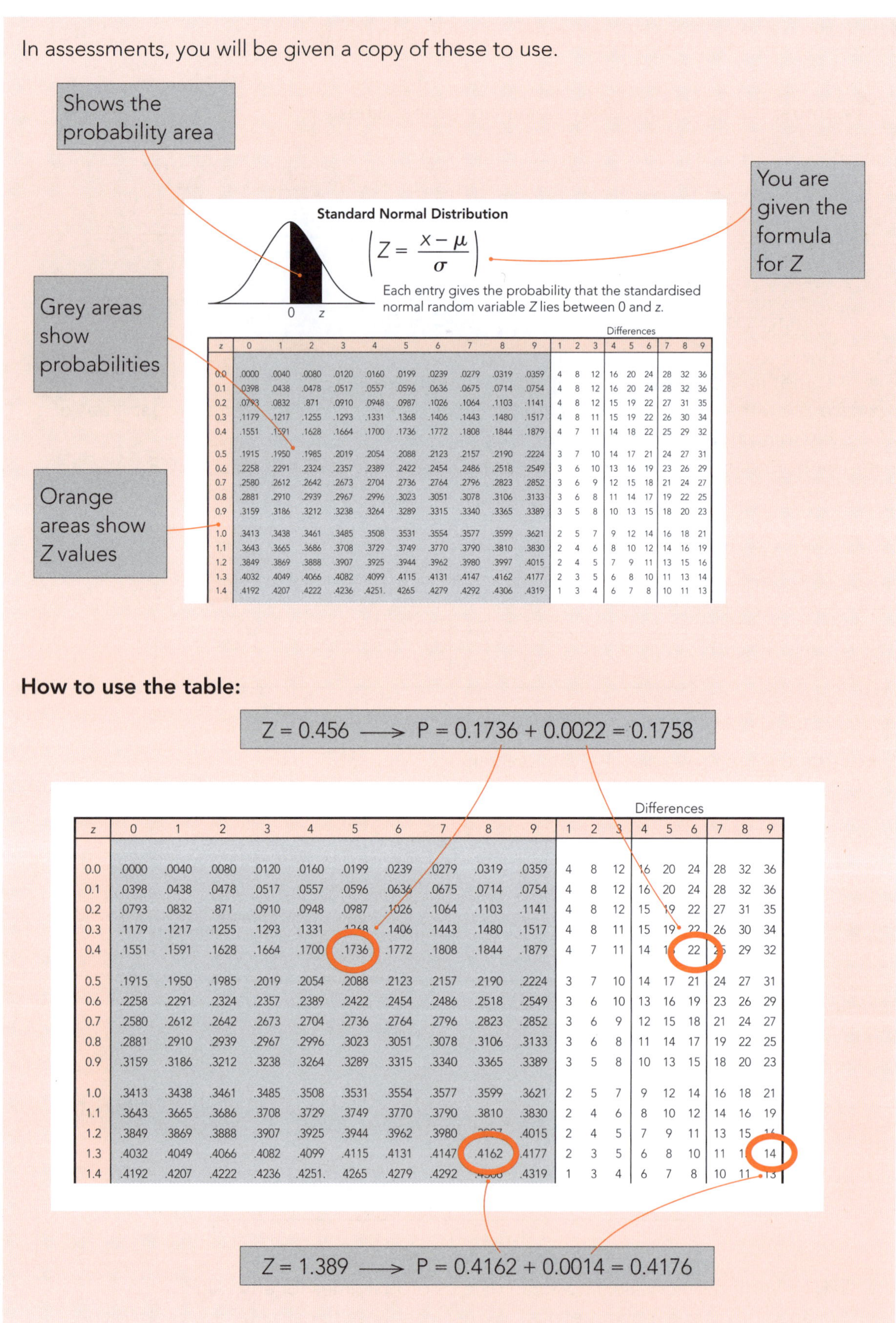

z	0	1	2	3	4	5	6	7	8	9	1	2	3	4	5	6	7	8	9
											Differences								
0.0	.0000	.0040	.0080	.0120	.0160	.0199	.0239	.0279	.0319	.0359	4	8	12	16	20	24	28	32	36
0.1	.0398	.0438	.0478	.0517	.0557	.0596	.0636	.0675	.0714	.0754	4	8	12	16	20	24	28	32	36
0.2	.0793	.0832	.871	.0910	.0948	.0987	.1026	.1064	.1103	.1141	4	8	12	15	19	22	27	31	35
0.3	.1179	.1217	.1255	.1293	.1331	.1368	.1406	.1443	.1480	.1517	4	8	11	15	19	22	26	30	34
0.4	.1551	.1591	.1628	.1664	.1700	.1736	.1772	.1808	.1844	.1879	4	7	11	14	18	22	25	29	32
0.5	.1915	.1950	.1985	.2019	.2054	.2088	.2123	.2157	.2190	.2224	3	7	10	14	17	21	24	27	31
0.6	.2258	.2291	.2324	.2357	.2389	.2422	.2454	.2486	.2518	.2549	3	6	10	13	16	19	23	26	29
0.7	.2580	.2612	.2642	.2673	.2704	.2736	.2764	.2796	.2823	.2852	3	6	9	12	15	18	21	24	27
0.8	.2881	.2910	.2939	.2967	.2996	.3023	.3051	.3078	.3106	.3133	3	6	8	11	14	17	19	22	25
0.9	.3159	.3186	.3212	.3238	.3264	.3289	.3315	.3340	.3365	.3389	3	5	8	10	13	15	18	20	23
1.0	.3413	.3438	.3461	.3485	.3508	.3531	.3554	.3577	.3599	.3621	2	5	7	9	12	14	16	18	21
1.1	.3643	.3665	.3686	.3708	.3729	.3749	.3770	.3790	.3810	.3830	2	4	6	8	10	12	14	16	19
1.2	.3849	.3869	.3888	.3907	.3925	.3944	.3962	.3980	.3997	.4015	2	4	5	7	9	11	13	15	16
1.3	.4032	.4049	.4066	.4082	.4099	.4115	.4131	.4147	.4162	.4177	2	3	5	6	8	10	11	13	14
1.4	.4192	.4207	.4222	.4236	.4251.	4265	.4279	.4292	.4306	.4319	1	3	4	6	7	8	10	11	13

How to use the table:

$Z = 0.456 \longrightarrow P = 0.1736 + 0.0022 = 0.1758$

z	0	1	2	3	4	5	6	7	8	9	1	2	3	4	5	6	7	8	9
											Differences								
0.0	.0000	.0040	.0080	.0120	.0160	.0199	.0239	.0279	.0319	.0359	4	8	12	16	20	24	28	32	36
0.1	.0398	.0438	.0478	.0517	.0557	.0596	.0636	.0675	.0714	.0754	4	8	12	16	20	24	28	32	36
0.2	.0793	.0832	.871	.0910	.0948	.0987	.1026	.1064	.1103	.1141	4	8	12	15	19	22	27	31	35
0.3	.1179	.1217	.1255	.1293	.1331	.1368	.1406	.1443	.1480	.1517	4	8	11	15	19	22	26	30	34
0.4	.1551	.1591	.1628	.1664	.1700	.1736	.1772	.1808	.1844	.1879	4	7	11	14	18	22	25	29	32
0.5	.1915	.1950	.1985	.2019	.2054	.2088	.2123	.2157	.2190	.2224	3	7	10	14	17	21	24	27	31
0.6	.2258	.2291	.2324	.2357	.2389	.2422	.2454	.2486	.2518	.2549	3	6	10	13	16	19	23	26	29
0.7	.2580	.2612	.2642	.2673	.2704	.2736	.2764	.2796	.2823	.2852	3	6	9	12	15	18	21	24	27
0.8	.2881	.2910	.2939	.2967	.2996	.3023	.3051	.3078	.3106	.3133	3	6	8	11	14	17	19	22	25
0.9	.3159	.3186	.3212	.3238	.3264	.3289	.3315	.3340	.3365	.3389	3	5	8	10	13	15	18	20	23
1.0	.3413	.3438	.3461	.3485	.3508	.3531	.3554	.3577	.3599	.3621	2	5	7	9	12	14	16	18	21
1.1	.3643	.3665	.3686	.3708	.3729	.3749	.3770	.3790	.3810	.3830	2	4	6	8	10	12	14	16	19
1.2	.3849	.3869	.3888	.3907	.3925	.3944	.3962	.3980	.3997	.4015	2	4	5	7	9	11	13	15	16
1.3	.4032	.4049	.4066	.4082	.4099	.4115	.4131	.4147	.4162	.4177	2	3	5	6	8	10	11	13	14
1.4	.4192	.4207	.4222	.4236	.4251.	4265	.4279	.4292	.4306	.4319	1	3	4	6	7	8	10	11	13

$Z = 1.389 \longrightarrow P = 0.4162 + 0.0014 = 0.4176$

ISBN: 9780170354240

Given the following Z values, find the probabilities.

1 $Z = 1.3 \longrightarrow P(x) =$

2 $Z = 2.75 \longrightarrow P(x) =$

3 $Z = 1.96 \longrightarrow P(x) =$

4 $Z = 1.645 \longrightarrow P(x) =$

5 $Z = 3.258 \longrightarrow P(x) =$

6 $Z = 0.678 \longrightarrow P(x) =$

7 $Z = 2.028 \longrightarrow P(x) =$

8 $Z = 3.9 \longrightarrow P(x) =$

9 $Z = 2.809 \longrightarrow P(x) =$

10 $Z = 0.008 \longrightarrow P(x) =$

Calculating a probability on the right side of the curve

Example: The weights of students' backpacks are found to be normally distributed with a mean of 3.3 kg and a standard deviation of 0.3 kg. Calculate the probability that a backpack weighs between 3.3 kg and 4.0 kg.

Step 1: Draw the picture.

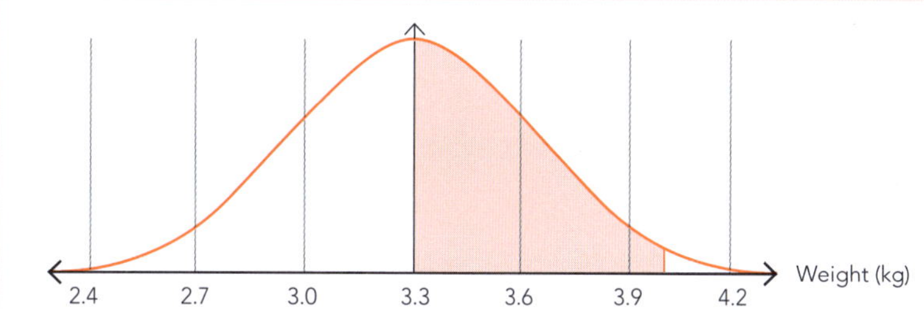

Step 2: Calculate the Z value.

$$Z = \frac{x - \mu}{\sigma} = \frac{4 - 3.3}{0.3} = 2.333$$

Always round Z values to 3 d.p.

Step 3: Look up the tables to find the probability.

$$Z = 2.333 \longrightarrow P = 0.4902$$

Step 4: Write your answer as a sentence and in context.
The probability that a backpack weighs between 3.3 kg and 4.0 kg is 0.4902.

ISBN: 9780170354240

Calculate the following probabilities.

1 The mean distance jumped in a school long-jump competition was 170 cm, with a standard deviation of 15 cm. Calculate the probability that Jac jumped between 170 cm and 200 cm.

Step 1:

Step 2:

Step 3:

Step 4:

2 The average number of ice creams sold each day from a mobile van is 278, with a standard deviation of 13. Calculate the probability that between 278 and 300 are sold in a day.

Step 1:

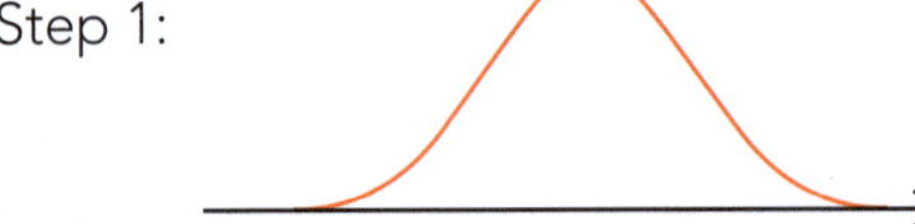

Step 2:

Step 3:

Step 4:

3 The average rainfall for a town is 960 mm, with a standard deviation of 22 mm. Calculate the probability that this town receives between 960 mm and 1000 mm in a year.

ISBN: 9780170354240

Probabilities below a value

Remember that the curve is symmetrical, so the area to the left of the mean is 0.5.

Example: The weights of students' backpacks are found to be normally distributed with a mean of 3.3 kg and a standard deviation of 0.3 kg. Calculate the probability that a backpack weighs less than 3.5 kg.

Step 1: Draw the picture.

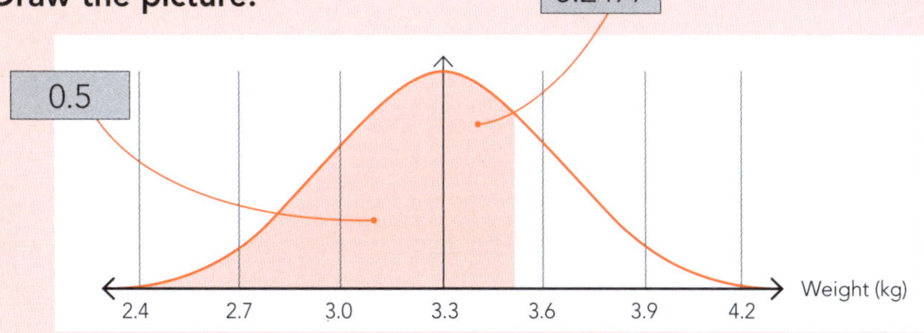

Step 2: Calculate the Z value.

$$Z = \frac{x - \mu}{\sigma} = \frac{3.5 - 3.3}{0.3} = 0.667$$

Remember to round to 3 dp

Step 3: Look up the tables to find the probability.

$$Z = 0.667 \longrightarrow P(3.3 < x < 3.5) = 0.2477$$

$$\mathbf{P(x < 3.5) = 0.5 + 0.2477 = 0.7477}$$

Step 4: Write your answer as a sentence and in context.
The probability that a backpack weighs less than 3.5 kg is 0.7477.

Try for yourself:

The distances jumped in a school long-jump competition have a mean of 170 cm with a standard deviation of 15 cm. Calculate the probability that a student jumped less than 200 cm.

Step 1:

Step 2:

Step 3:

Step 4:

ISBN: 9780170354240

Probabilities from the right tail of the curve

Example: The weights of students' backpacks are found to be normally distributed with a mean of 3.3 kg and a standard deviation of 0.3 kg. Calculate the probability that a backpack weighs more than 3.7 kg.

Step 1: Draw the picture.

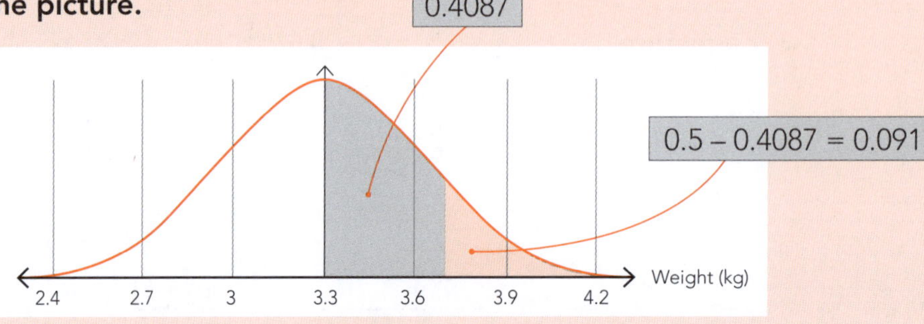

Step 2: Calculate the *Z* value.

$$Z = \frac{x - \mu}{\sigma} = \frac{3.7 - 3.3}{0.3} = 1.333$$

Step 3: Look up the tables to find the probability.

$$Z = 1.333 \longrightarrow P(3.3 < x < 3.7) = 0.4087$$

$$\mathbf{P(x > 3.7) = 0.5 - 0.4087 = 0.0913}$$

Step 4: Write your answer as a sentence and in context.
The probability that a backpack weighs more than 3.7 kg is 0.0913.

Try for yourself:

The distances jumped in a school long-jump competition have a mean of 170 cm with a standard deviation of 15 cm. Calculate the probability that a student jumped over 180 cm.

Step 1:

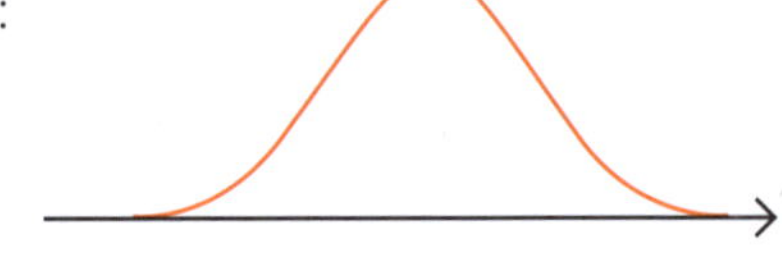

Step 2:

Step 3:

Step 4:

ISBN: 9780170354240

Calculate the following probabilities.

1 In 2014, Americans spent on average 40 minutes per day on social media. If the distribution of these times is normally distributed and the standard deviation is 9.7 minutes:

a Calculate the probability an American spends spends more than an hour a day on social media.

b Calculate the probability that an American spends less than 50 minutes a day on social media.

2 If the average distance run by a scrum half during a rugby game is 6.5 km, and the distances are normally distributed and the standard deviation is 1.4 km:

a Calculate the probability that a scrum half runs less than 7 km during a game.

b Calculate the probability that a scrum half runs more than 8 km during a game.

ISBN: 9780170354240

Probabilities on the left of the curve

Remember that the curve is symmetrical, so the area to the left is a reflection of that on the right. When you look up the probability in the tables, ignore the negative sign in front of the *Z* value.

Example: The weights of students' backpacks are found to be normally distributed with a mean of 3.3 kg and a standard deviation of 0.3 kg. Calculate the probability that a backpack weighs between 2.7 kg and 3.3 kg.

Step 1: Draw the picture.

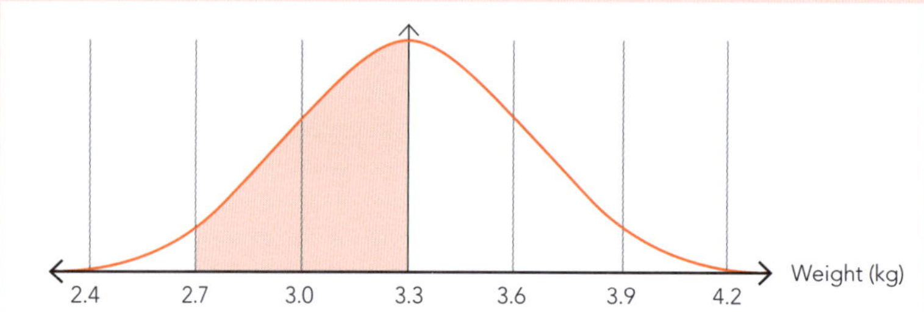

Step 2: Calculate the *Z* value.

$$Z = \frac{x - \mu}{\sigma} = \frac{2.7 - 3.3}{0.3} = -2$$

Step 3: Look up the tables to find the probability.

$$Z = 2 \longrightarrow \mathbf{P(2.7 < x < 3.3) = 0.4772}$$

Step 4: Write your answer as a sentence and in context.
The probability that a backpack weighs between 2.7 kg and 3.3 kg is 0.4772.

Try for yourself:

The distances jumped in a school long-jump competition have a mean of 170 cm with a standard deviation of 15 cm. Calculate the probability that a student jumped between 150 cm and 170 cm.

Step 1:

Step 2:

Step 3:

Step 4:

 ISBN: 9780170354240

Probabilities from the left tail of the curve

Remember that the curve is symmetrical, so we can reflect probabilities from the left to the right.

Example: The weights of students' backpacks are found to be normally distributed with a mean of 3.3 kg and a standard deviation of 0.3 kg. Calculate the probability that a backpack weighs less than 2.8 kg.

Step 1: Draw the picture.

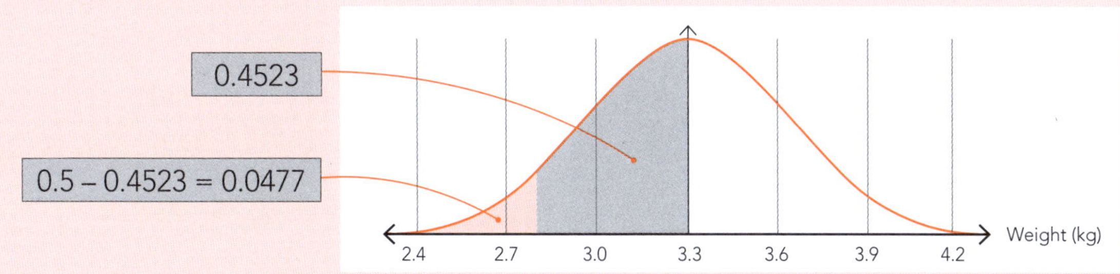

Step 2: Calculate the *Z* value.

$$Z = \frac{x - \mu}{\sigma} = \frac{2.8 - 3.3}{0.3} = -1.667$$

Step 3: Look up the tables to find the probability.

$$Z = 1.667 \longrightarrow P(2.8 < x < 3.3) = 0.4523$$

$$\mathbf{P(x < 2.8) = 0.5 - 0.4523 = 0.0477}$$

Step 4: Write your answer as a sentence and in context.
The probability that a backpack weighs less than 2.8 kg is 0.0477.

Try for yourself:

The distances jumped in a school long-jump competition have a mean of 170 cm with a standard deviation of 15 cm. Calculate the probability that a student jumped less than 140 cm.

Step 1:

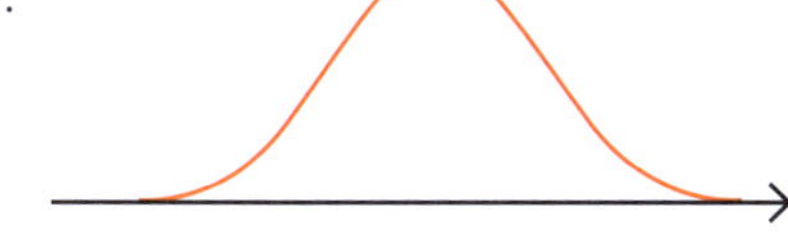

Step 2:

Step 3:

Step 4:

ISBN 9780170354240

Calculate the following probabilities.

1 In 2014, Americans spent on average 40 minutes per day on social media. If the distribution of these times is normally distributed and the standard deviation is 9.7 minutes:

a Calculate the probability that an American spends less than 15 minutes a day on social media.

b Calculate the probability that an American spends between 30 minutes and 40 minutes a day on social media.

2 If the average distance run by a scrum half during a rugby game is 6.5 km, and the distances are normally distributed and the standard deviation is 1.4 km:

a Calculate the probability that a scrum half runs less than 4 km.

b Calculate the probability that a scrum half runs between 6 km and 6.5 km.

 ISBN: 9780170354240

Probabilities from both sides of the curve

Example: The weights of students' backpacks are found to be normally distributed with a mean of 3.3 kg and a standard deviation of 0.3 kg. Calculate the probability that a backpack weighs between 2.9 kg and 3.6 kg.

Step 1: Draw the picture.

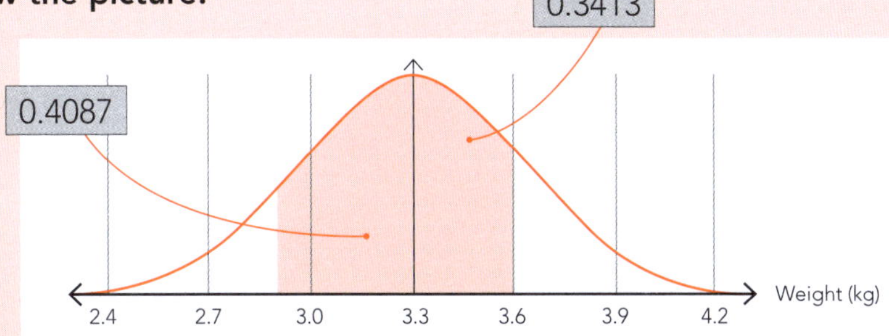

Step 2: Calculate the *Z* value.

$$Z_{2.9} = \frac{x-\mu}{\sigma} = \frac{2.9-3.3}{0.3} = -1.333 \qquad Z_{3.6} = \frac{x-\mu}{\sigma} = \frac{3.6-3.3}{0.3} = 1$$

Step 3: Look up the tables to find the probability.

$Z = 1.333 \longrightarrow P(2.9 < x < 3.3) = 0.4087$ and $Z = 1 \longrightarrow P(3.3 < x < 3.6) = 0.3413$

$$\mathbf{P(2.9 < x < 3.6) = 0.4087 + 0.3413 = 0.75}$$

Add the areas

Step 4: Write your answer as a sentence and in context.
The probability that a backpack weighs between than 2.9 kg and 3.6 kg is 0.75.

Try for yourself:

The distances jumped in a school long-jump competition have a mean of 170 cm with a standard deviation of 15 cm. Calculate the probability that a student jumped between 155 and 180 cm.

Step 1:

Step 2:

Step 3:

Step 4:

ISBN: 9780170354240

Probabilities from two tails of the curve

Remember that the curve is symmetrical, so we can reflect probabilities from the left to the right.

Example: The weights of students' backpacks are found to be normally distributed with a mean of 3.3 kg and a standard deviation of 0.3 kg. Calculate the probability that a backpack weighs less than 2.8 kg or more than 3.6 kg.

Step 1: Draw the picture.

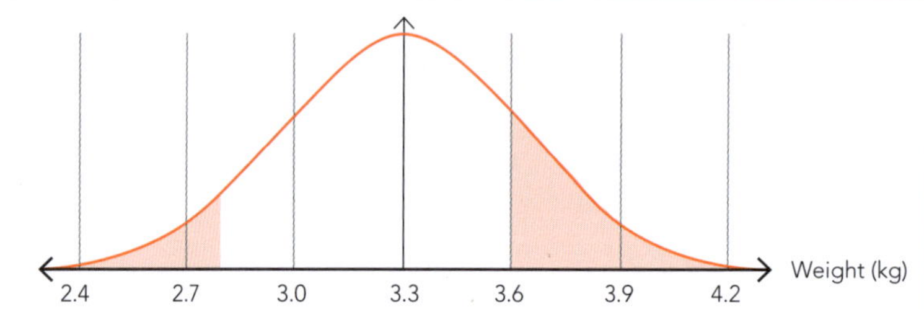

Step 2: Calculate the *Z* value.

$$Z_{2.8} = \frac{x-\mu}{\sigma} = \frac{2.8-3.3}{0.3} = -1.667 \qquad Z_{3.6} = \frac{x-\mu}{\sigma} = \frac{3.6-3.3}{0.3} = 1$$

Step 3: Look up the tables to find the probability.

$Z = 1.667 \longrightarrow P(2.8 < x < 3.3) = 0.4523$ and $Z = 1 \longrightarrow P(3.3 < x < 3.6) = 0.3413$

$$\mathbf{P(x < 2.8 \text{ or } x > 3.6) = (0.5 - 0.4523) + (0.5 - 0.3413) = 0.2064}$$

Add the areas

Step 4: Write your answer as a sentence and in context.
The probability that a backpack weighs less than 2.8 kg or more than 3.6 kg is 0.2064.

Try for yourself:

The distances jumped in a school long-jump competition have a mean of 170 cm with a standard deviation of 15 cm. Calculate the probability that a student jumped less than 150 cm or more than 200 cm.

Step 1:

Step 2:

Step 3:

Step 4:

ISBN: 9780170354240

Calculate the following probabilities.

1 In 2014, Americans spent on average 40 minutes per day on social media. If the distribution of these times is normally distributed and the standard deviation is 9.7 minutes:

a Calculate the probability that an American spends between 30 and 55 minutes on social media in a day.

b Calculate the probability that an American spends less than 20 or more than 70 minutes on social media in a day.

2 If the average distance run by a scrum half during a rugby game is 6.5 km, and the distances are normally distributed and the standard deviation is 1.4 km:

a Calculate the probability that a scrum half runs less than 6 km or more than 8 km in a rugby game.

b Calculate the probability that a scrum half runs between 5.5 km and 8.5 km during a game.

ISBN: 9780170354240

Calculating probabilities by difference

Example: The weights of students' backpacks are found to be normally distributed with a mean of 3.3 kg and a standard deviation of 0.3 kg. Calculate the probability that a backpack weighs between 2.7 kg and 3.1 kg.

Step 1: Draw the picture.

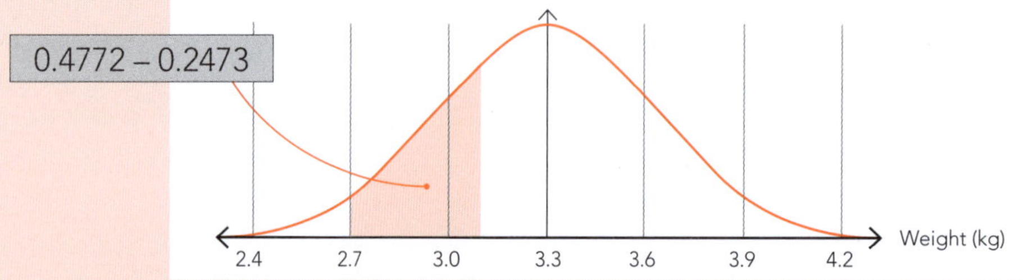

Step 2: Calculate the *Z* value.

$$Z_{2.7} = \frac{x-\mu}{\sigma} = \frac{2.7-3.3}{0.3} = -2 \qquad Z_{3.1} = \frac{x-\mu}{\sigma} = \frac{3.1-3.3}{0.3} = -0.667$$

Step 3: Look up the tables to find the probability.

$Z = 2 \longrightarrow P(2.7 < x < 3.3) = 0.4772$ and $Z = 0.667 \longrightarrow P(3.1 < x < 3.3) = 0.2477$

$$\mathbf{P(2.7 < x < 3.1) = 0.4772 - 0.2473 = 0.2299}$$

Subtract the areas

Step 4: Write your answer as a sentence and in context.
The probability that a backpack weighs between 2.7 kg and 3.1 kg is 0.2299.

Try for yourself:

The distances jumped in a school long-jump competition have a mean of 170 cm with a standard deviation of 15 cm. Calculate the probability that a student jumped between 160 cm and 162 cm.

Step 1:

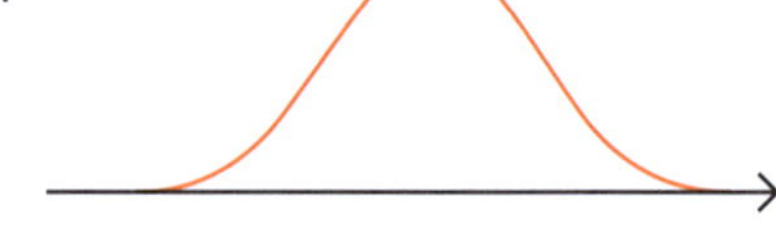

Step 2:

Step 3:

Step 4:

ISBN: 9780170354240

Using a graphics calculator to calculate probabilities

1 Question on page 32:
The weights of students' backpacks are found to be normally distributed with a mean of 3.3 kg and a standard deviation of 0.3 kg. Calculate the probability that a backpack weighs between 2.7 kg and 3.1 kg.

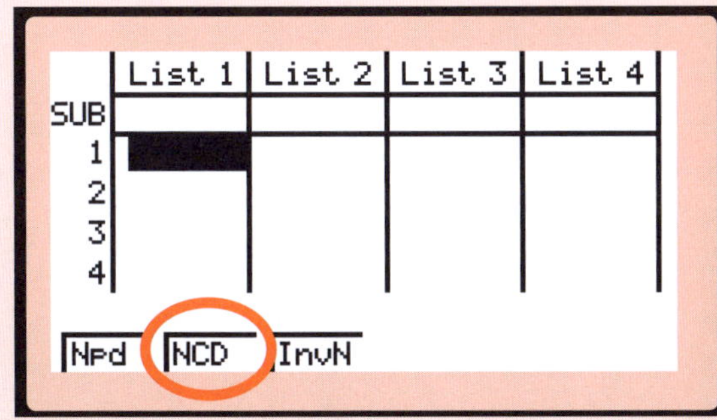

→ **Menu**
→ **Stat**
→ **Dist**
→ **NORM**
→ **Ncd**

Make sure the setting is Var, not List.
Note: This will revert back to List when your calculator is reset.

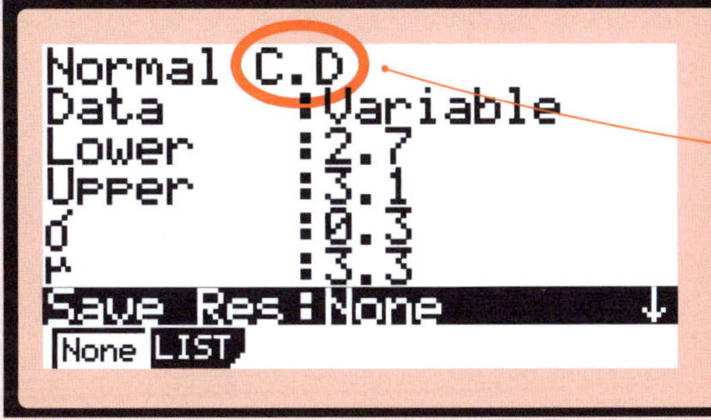

Calculates probability **between** 2.7 and 3.1 kg

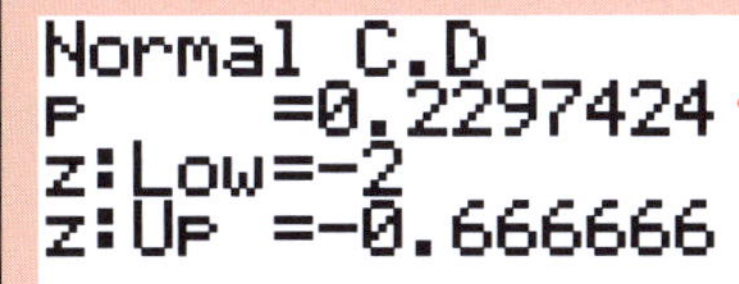

This is your answer (which may differ slightly from the answer you get using tables)

2 Question on page 24:
The weights of students' backpacks are found to be normally distributed with a mean of 3.3 kg and a standard deviation of 0.3 kg. Calculate the probability that a backpack weighs more than 3.7 kg.

Your upper limit needs to be something large

Normal C.D
p =0.09121121
z:Low=1.33333333
z:Up =33322.3333

This is your answer

ISBN: 9780170354240

Mixing it up

1 The estimated average life span of a kakapo (a rare New Zealand ground-living parrot) is 95 years. If the life spans are normally distributed, with a standard deviation of 11 years:

a Calculate the percentage of kakapo that lives to more than 120 years old.

b Calculate the probability that a kakapo lives between 90 and 100 years.

c Calculate the probability that a kakapo lives for longer than 80 years.

d In March 2014 there were 130 living kakapo. How many would you expect to die before they are 70 years old?

ISBN: 9780170354240

2 An energy-saver light bulb is advertised as having an average life of 10,000 hours with a standard deviation of 700 hours. If the life spans are normally distributed:

a Calculate the probability that a bulb lasts longer than 11,000 hours.

b Calculate the probability that a bulb lasts between 9500 and 11,000 hours.

c Calculate the probability that a bulb lasts between 8500 and 9500 hours.

d The company gives a replacement guarantee that their bulbs last longer than 8000 hours. If an outlet sells 950 of these bulbs, how many bulbs can it expect to replace under the terms of the guarantee?

ISBN: 9780170354240

3 The machine which fills soft drink bottles is set so that the mean volume in each bottle is 1004 mL, with a standard deviation of 1.6 mL. The volumes are normally distributed.

a Calculate the probability that a bottle contains more than 1008 mL.

b Calculate the probability that a bottle contains between 1002 mL and 1006 mL.

c What percentage of bottles would you expect to contain less than 1005 mL?

d The label on the bottles states that each bottle contains one litre of soft drink. What percentage of the bottles contains less than one litre? If 1.8 million bottles of this soft drink are produced each year, calculate the number of these bottles which contain less than one litre.

ISBN: 9780170354240

4 The time taken for purchasers to assemble an 'Easikit' bookshelf has a mean of 98 minutes, with a standard deviation of 14 minutes. If these times are normally distributed:

a Calculate the probability that a purchaser took between 98 and 112 minutes to assemble the bookshelf.

b Calculate the probability that a purchaser took less than 80 minutes to assemble the bookshelf.

c Calculate the probability that a purchaser took between 90 and 110 minutes to assemble the bookshelf. What percentage of purchasers assembled it within this interval?

d If 380 bookshelves were sold, how many purchasers would you expect to take more than two hours to assemble the bookshelf?

ISBN: 9780170354240

2 Inverse normal calculations

Inverse normal calculations are used when:

- we know the probability of an event
- we don't know the value of one of the parameters.

Then:

- we use the tables to look up the value of Z which corresponds to the probability
- we use the formula for Z to calculate the missing parameter.

Using a probability to find Z

How to use the tables:

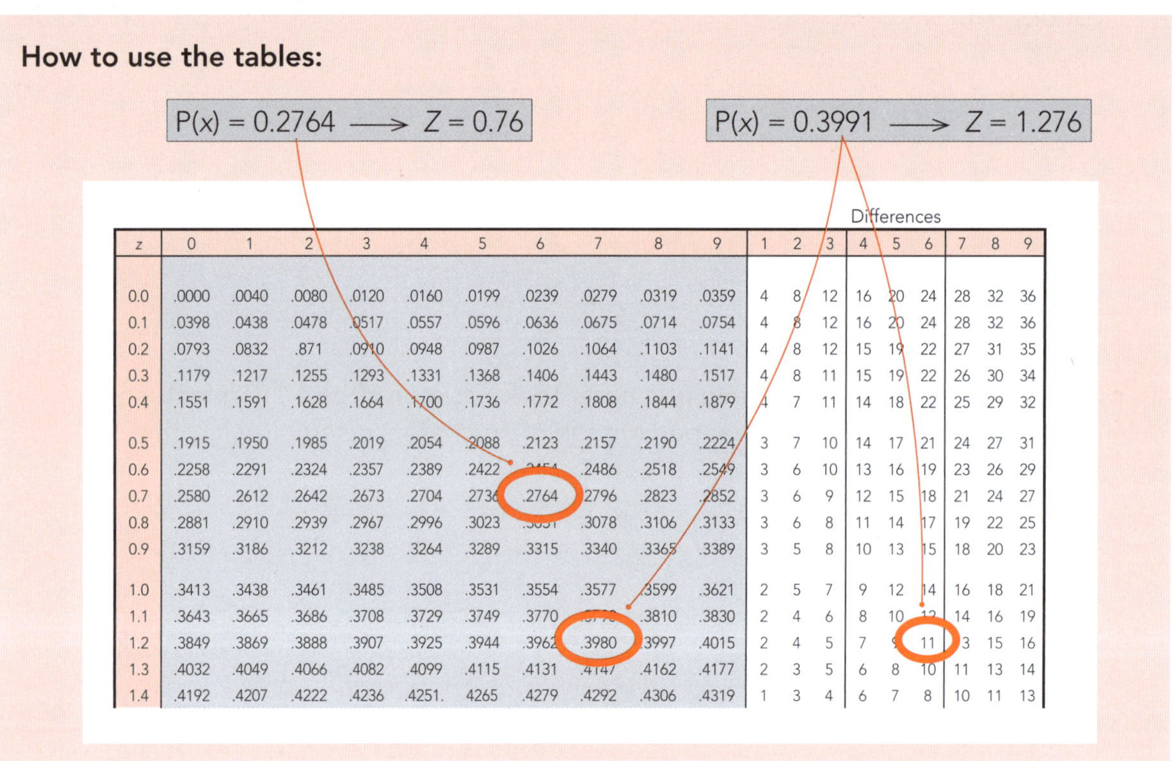

P(x) = 0.2764 ⟶ Z = 0.76

P(x) = 0.3991 ⟶ Z = 1.276

z	0	1	2	3	4	5	6	7	8	9	Differences 1	2	3	4	5	6	7	8	9
0.0	.0000	.0040	.0080	.0120	.0160	.0199	.0239	.0279	.0319	.0359	4	8	12	16	20	24	28	32	36
0.1	.0398	.0438	.0478	.0517	.0557	.0596	.0636	.0675	.0714	.0754	4	8	12	16	20	24	28	32	36
0.2	.0793	.0832	.871	.0910	.0948	.0987	.1026	.1064	.1103	.1141	4	8	12	15	19	22	27	31	35
0.3	.1179	.1217	.1255	.1293	.1331	.1368	.1406	.1443	.1480	.1517	4	8	11	15	19	22	26	30	34
0.4	.1551	.1591	.1628	.1664	.1700	.1736	.1772	.1808	.1844	.1879	4	7	11	14	18	22	25	29	32
0.5	.1915	.1950	.1985	.2019	.2054	.2088	.2123	.2157	.2190	.2224	3	7	10	14	17	21	24	27	31
0.6	.2258	.2291	.2324	.2357	.2389	.2422	[illegible]	.2486	.2518	.2549	3	6	10	13	16	19	23	26	29
0.7	.2580	.2612	.2642	.2673	.2704	.2736	.2764	.2796	.2823	.2852	3	6	9	12	15	18	21	24	27
0.8	.2881	.2910	.2939	.2967	.2996	.3023	[illegible]	.3078	.3106	.3133	3	6	8	11	14	17	19	22	25
0.9	.3159	.3186	.3212	.3238	.3264	.3289	.3315	.3340	.3365	.3389	3	5	8	10	13	15	18	20	23
1.0	.3413	.3438	.3461	.3485	.3508	.3531	.3554	.3577	.3599	.3621	2	5	7	9	12	14	16	18	21
1.1	.3643	.3665	.3686	.3708	.3729	.3749	.3770	[illegible]	.3810	.3830	2	4	6	8	10	[illegible]	14	16	19
1.2	.3849	.3869	.3888	.3907	.3925	.3944	.3962	.3980	.3997	.4015	2	4	5	7	9	11	[illegible]	15	16
1.3	.4032	.4049	.4066	.4082	.4099	.4115	.4131	.4147	.4162	.4177	2	3	5	6	8	10	11	13	14
1.4	.4192	.4207	.4222	.4236	.4251.	4265	.4279	.4292	.4306	.4319	1	3	4	6	7	8	10	11	13

Look up the values of Z for each of the following probabilities.

1 P(x) = 0.4922 ⟶ Z = ______________

2 P(x) = 0.0636 ⟶ Z = ______________

3 P(x) = 0.4987 ⟶ Z = ______________

4 P(x) = 0.3425 ⟶ Z = ______________

5 P(x) = 0.4753 ⟶ Z = ______________

6 P(x) = 0.2085 ⟶ Z = ______________

7 P(x) = 0.4606 ⟶ Z = ______________

8 P(x) = 0.4840 ⟶ Z = ______________

9 P(x) = 0.0434 ⟶ Z = ______________

10 P(x) = 0.4914 ⟶ Z = ______________

ISBN: 9780170354240

Using Z to calculate the value of x — where Z is positive

Example: The weights of students' backpacks are found to be normally distributed with a mean of 3.3 kg and a standard deviation of 0.4 kg. Above what weight (w) do 20% of backpacks lie?

Step 1: Draw the picture.

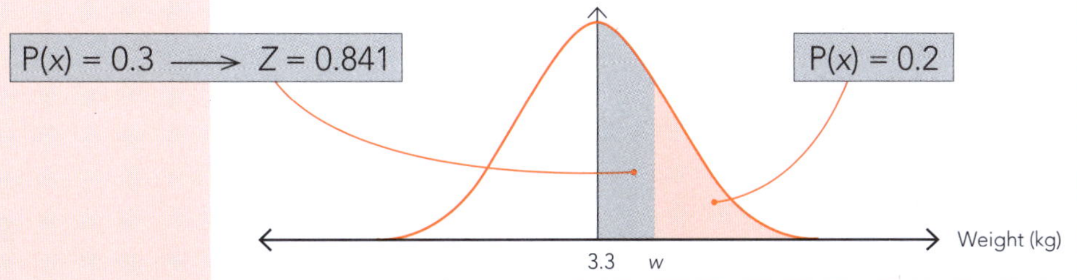

Step 2: Use the probability to look up the Z value.

$P(x > w) = 0.2 \longrightarrow P(3.3 < x < w) = 0.5 - 0.2 = 0.3$
So $Z = 0.841$

Step 3: Use the Z value to calculate the value of x.

$$Z = \frac{w - 3.3}{0.4} = 0.841 \longrightarrow w - 3.3 = 0.3364, \text{ so } w = 3.6364 \text{ kg}$$

Step 4: Write your answer as a sentence and in context.
Twenty per cent of backpacks weigh more than 3.6364 kg.

Step 5: Does my answer make sense?
Yes, because 3.6364 is above the mean of 3.3 kg.

Calculate the values of x in the following.

1 The distances jumped in a school long-jump competition have a mean of 170 cm with a standard deviation of 15 cm. The top 20% of competitors will get a bonus point for their house. What is the minimum distance jumped that will earn a bonus point?

Step 1:

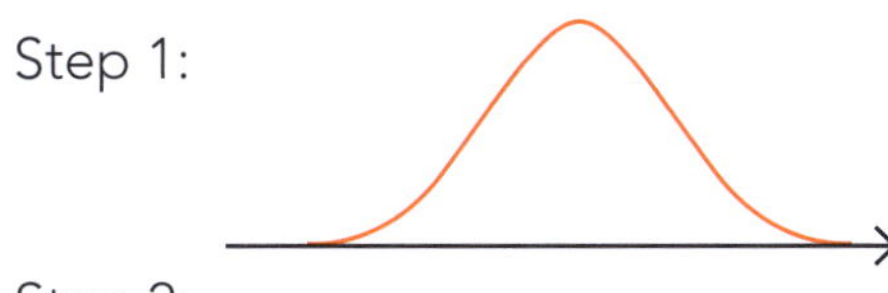

Step 2:

Step 3:

Step 4:

Step 5:

ISBN: 9780170354240

2 It is known that weights of apples produced per tree in an orchard are normally distributed with a mean of 120 kg, and the standard deviation is 23 kg. Calculate the upper quartile (above which 25% of values lie).

Step 1:

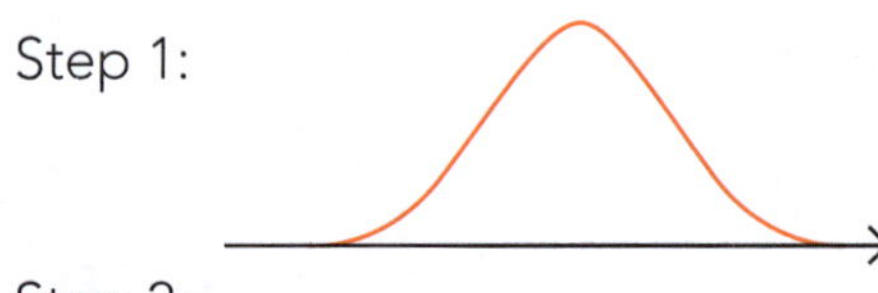

Step 2:

Step 3:

Step 4:

Step 5:

3 A music examination is marked out of 150. The marks are normally distributed with a mean of 95 and a standard deviation of 15. The top 5% of students are awarded distinction. Calculate the lowest mark that would qualify for distinction.

4 A farmer harvests his courgettes when their mean weight is 150 g, with a standard deviation of 55 g. Assume that the distribution of the courgette weights is normal. The largest courgettes return a much lower price because they are classified as marrows. If 5% of his crop consists of marrows, calculate the minimum weight for a courgette to be classified as a marrow.

ISBN: 9780170354240

Using Z to calculate the value of x — where Z is negative

Example: The weights of students' backpacks are found to be normally distributed with a mean of 3.3 kg and a standard deviation of 0.4 kg. Below what weight (w) do 10% of backpacks lie?

Step 1: Draw the picture.

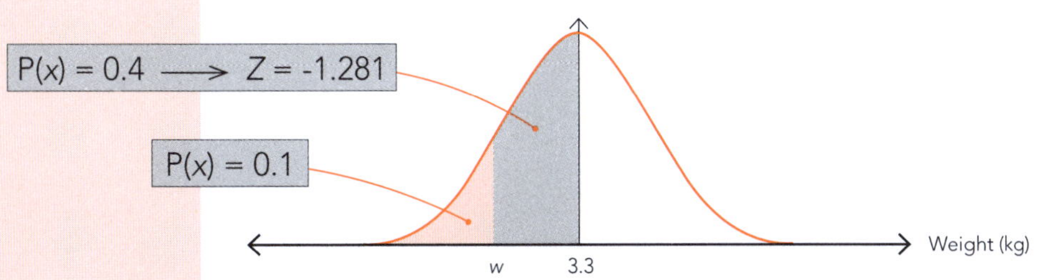

Step 2: Use the probability to look up the Z value.

$P(x < w) = 0.1 \longrightarrow P(w < x < 3.3) = 0.5 - 0.1 = 0.4$

So $Z = -1.281$ (Note: You could also use $Z = -1.282$)

Step 3: Use the Z value to calculate the value of x.

$$Z = \frac{w - 3.3}{0.4} = -1.281 \longrightarrow w - 3.3 = -0.5124, \text{ so } w = 2.7876 \text{ kg}$$

Step 4: Write your answer as a sentence and in context.

Ten per cent of backpacks weigh less than 2.787 kg.

Step 5: Does my answer make sense?

Yes, because 2.787 is below the mean of 3.3 kg.

Calculate the values of x in the following.

1 The distances jumped in a school long-jump competition have a mean of 170 cm with a standard deviation of 15 cm. The bottom 10% of competitors will be eliminated after the first round. What is the minimum distance jumped that will prevent elimination?

Step 1:

Step 2:

Step 3:

Step 4:

Step 5:

2 It is known that weights of apples produced per tree in an orchard are normally distributed with a mean of 120 kg, and the standard deviation is 23 kg. The orchardist wants to replace the least productive 20% of his trees. Calculate the minimum weight of apples that a tree must produce if it is to be kept.

Step 1:

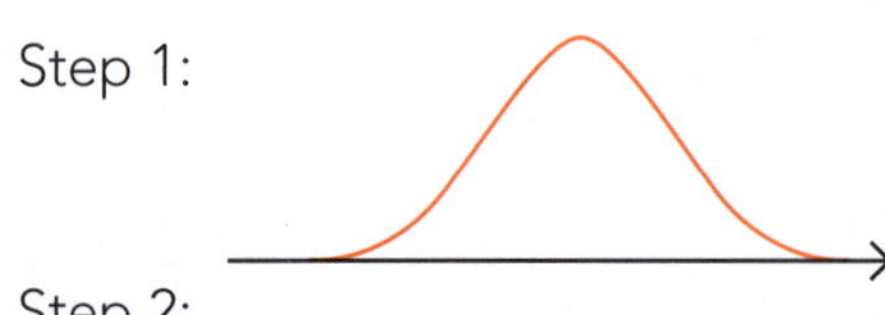

Step 2:

Step 3:

Step 4:

Step 5:

3 A music examination is marked out of 150. The marks are normally distributed with a mean of 95 and a standard deviation of 15. Those in the bottom 40% fail the examination. Calculate the highest mark that would result in a fail.

4 A plant nursery is growing seedlings of a new variety of matipo bushes. The 15% of seedlings which are shortest will be sold at sale price. The height of the seedlings is normally distributed with a mean of 53 cm and a standard deviation of 4.9 cm. Calculate the maximum height for the seedlings sold at sale price.

ISBN: 9780170354240

Using a graphics calculator to calculate inverse probabilities

This can be done ONLY for inverse probabilities where you are asked for the value of x, NOT where you need to find the mean or standard deviation.

1 Question on page 39:
The weights of students' backpacks are found to be normally distributed with a mean of 3.3 kg and a standard deviation of 0.4 kg. Above what weight do 20% of backpacks lie?

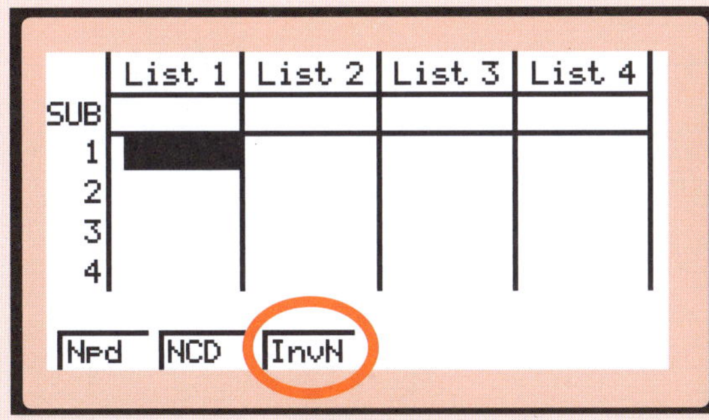

→ **Menu**
→ **Stat**
→ **Dist**
→ **Norm**
→ **InvN**

Make sure the setting is Var, not List.
Note: This will revert back to List when your calculator is reset.

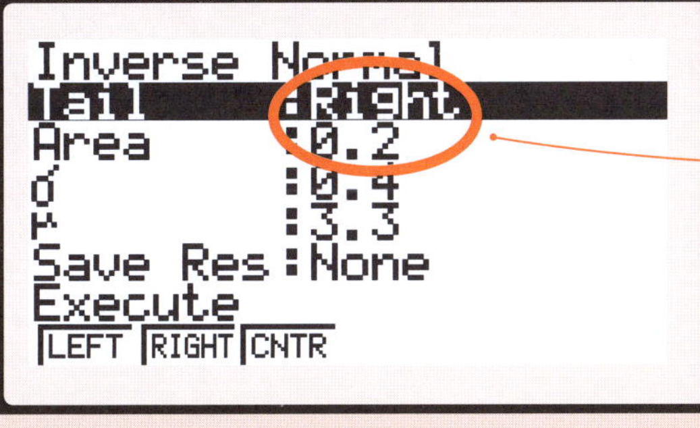

Calculates value of *x* which gives a probability of 0.2 on the **tail** to the **right** of the mean.

This is your answer (which may differ slightly from the answer you get using tables).

2 Question on page 41:
The weights of students' backpacks are found to be normally distributed with a mean of 3.3 kg and a standard deviation of 0.4 kg. Below what weight do 10% of backpacks lie?

Calculates the value of *x* which gives a probability of 0.1 on the **tail** to the **left** of the mean.

Inverse Normal
x=2.78737937

This is your answer.

ISBN: 9780170354240

Using Z to calculate the mean

Example: The weights of students' backpacks are found to be normally distributed with a standard deviation of 0.6 kg. If the probability that a backpack weighs more than 4.0 kg is 0.0179, calculate the mean weight of the backpacks.

Step 1: Draw the picture.

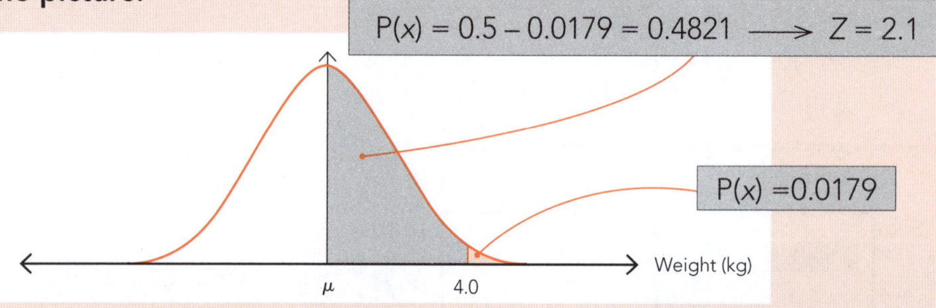

Step 2: Use the probability to look up the Z value.

$P(x > 4) = 0.0179 \longrightarrow P(\mu < x < 4) = 0.4821$
From the tables, $Z = 2.1$.

Remember tables give probabilities only for the area between μ and x:

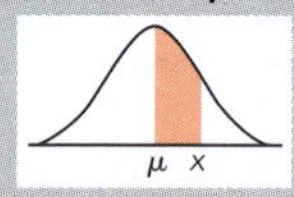

Step 3: Use the Z value to calculate the value of x.

$$Z = \frac{4-\mu}{0.6} = 2.1 \longrightarrow 4 - \mu = 1.26, \text{ so } \mu = 2.74 \text{ kg}$$

Step 4: Write your answer as a sentence and in context.
The mean weight for the backpacks is 2.74 kg.

Step 5: Does my answer make sense?
Yes, because 2.74 kg is less than 4 kg.

Calculate the mean in the following.

1 The distances jumped in a school long-jump competition are normally distributed with a standard deviation of 8 cm. If the probability that a student jumped less than 160 cm is 0.0062, calculate the mean length jumped.

Step 1:

Step 2:

Step 3:

Step 4:

Step 5:

ISBN: 9780170354240

2 A machine fills bags of popcorn. The weight of popcorn in the bags is normally distributed with a standard deviation of 1.5 g. If only 2% of bags contains more than 59 g of popcorn, calculate the mean weight that should be put in each bag.

Step 1:

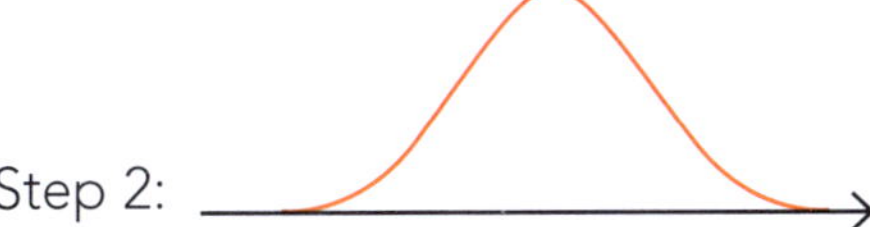

Step 2:

Step 3:

Step 4:

Step 5:

3 Another machine fills bags of rice which are supposed to contain 500 g. The machine is set so that exactly 5% of bags contain less than 500 g. The weights of the bags are normally distributed with a standard deviation of 1.2158 g. Calculate the mean weight of the bags.

4 The number of hairs on the heads of adults is normally distributed with a standard deviation of 19,500. If 90% of adults have fewer than 125,000 hairs, calculate the mean number of hairs on an adult head.

ISBN: 9780170354240

Using Z to calculate the standard deviation

Example: The weights of students' backpacks are found to be normally distributed with a mean of 3.3 kg. Calculate the standard deviation if the probability that a backpack weighs between 2.7 kg and 3.3 kg is 0.4332.

Step 1: Draw the picture.

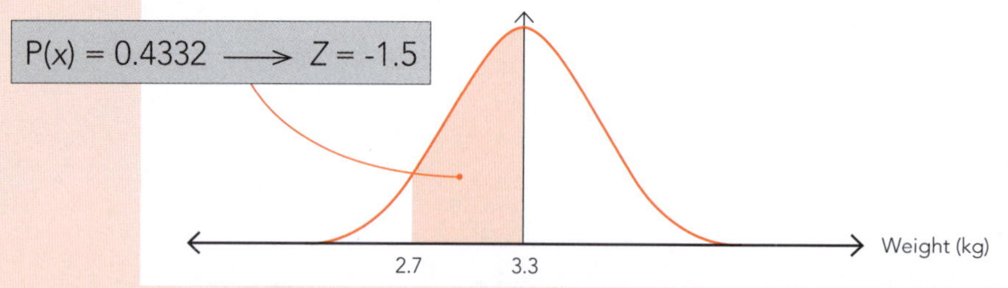

Step 2: Use the probability to look up the *Z* value.

$P(2.7 < x < 3.3) = 0.4332 \longrightarrow$ (from the tables) $Z = -1.5$

Step 3: Use the *Z* value to calculate the value of x.

$$Z = \frac{2.7 - 3.3}{\sigma} = -1.5 \longrightarrow \frac{-0.6}{\sigma} = -1.5, \text{ so } \sigma = 0.4 \text{ kg}$$

Step 4: Write your answer as a sentence and in context.
The standard deviation for the backpack weights is 0.4 kg.

Step 5: Does my answer make sense?
Yes, because 0.4 x 1.5 = 0.6 kg, which is 3.3 – 2.7 kg.

Calculate the standard deviation in the following.

1 The distances jumped in a school long-jump competition have a mean of 170 cm. If the probability that a student jumped between 170 cm and 188 cm is 0.3849, calculate the standard deviation.

Step 1:

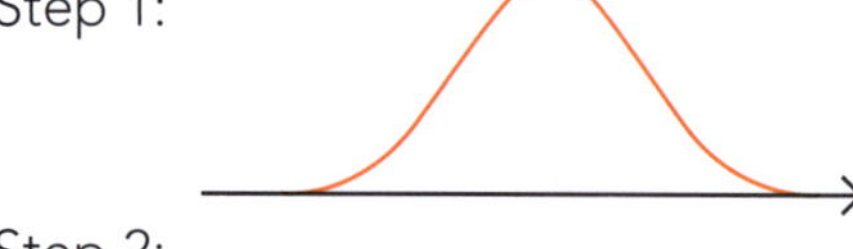

Step 2:

Step 3:

Step 4:

Step 5:

ISBN: 9780170354240

2 A species of moa has normally distributed weights with a mean of 170 kg. If a quarter of the individuals in this species weighed more than 185.5 kg, calculate the standard deviation for their weights.

Step 1:

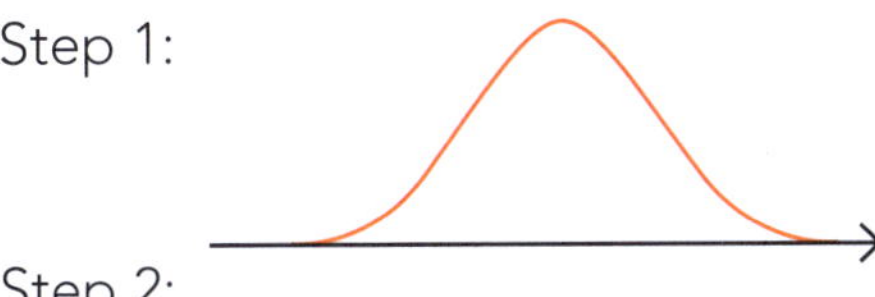

Step 2:

Step 3:

Step 4:

Step 5:

3 A farmer harvests his courgettes when their mean weight is 150 g. Assume that the distribution of the courgette weights is normal. Courgettes smaller than 100 g attract a premium price as 'gourmet' courgettes. If 19% of his crop attracts this premium, calculate the standard deviation for his courgette weights.

4 A set of test marks is normally distributed, has a lower quartile of 47% and an upper quartile of 61%. Calculate the mean mark and the standard deviation.

ISBN: 9780170354240

Mixing it up

1 A colony of endangered New Zealand long tailed bats contains adults with normally distributed weights which have a mean of 9.4 g. The heaviest 10% of the bats in the colony weigh more than 9.9765 g.

a Calculate the standard deviation for their weights.

b Calculate the percentage of bats which weigh more than 9 g.

2 The lifespan of some male mosquitoes is normally distributed with a mean of six days and a standard deviation of 7.5 hours.

a Calculate the age below which the 30% of shortest-lived mosquitoes die.

b Calculate the upper and lower quartiles for the lifespan of these mosquitoes.

ISBN: 9780170354240

3 It is known that a machine dispenses olive oil into bottles in a normally distributed manner, with a standard deviation of 2.44 mL. The bottle-filling machine is to be set so that exactly 5% of bottles contains less than the advertised 500 mL.

a Calculate the mean volume of olive oil in each bottle that the machine will need to dispense.

b How many bottles in a batch of 5000 would be expected to contain more than 510 mL?

4 On average, adults have 100,000 km of blood vessels in their bodies. Assume that the length of blood vessels in adults is normally distributed.

a If 90% of people have less than 120,000 km of blood vessels, calculate the standard deviation for this distribution.

b Between what lengths would the middle 40% of people have in their bodies?

5 A fencing examination is marked out of 200. The marks are normally distributed with a mean of 130 and a standard deviation of 20.

a Those in the top 5% progress to a national competition. Calculate the lowest mark that would qualify for this.

b Those in the bottom 45% are not awarded a certificate. Calculate the highest mark that would result in no certificate being awarded.

6 The Amazon River pours millions of litres of fresh water per second into the Atlantic Ocean. Assume this flow is normally distributed with a standard deviation of 17.62 million litres.

a If the lower quartile for this distribution is 197.12 million litres, and the upper quartile is 220.88 million litres, calculate the mean volume of water poured into the Atlantic each second.

b If it is in flood 1% of the time, calculate the minimum volume that flows into the Atlantic during a flood.

ISBN: 9780170354240

7 A farmer harvests his courgettes when their mean weight is 150 g. Assume that the distribution of the courgette weights is normal.

a Courgettes smaller than 100 g attract a premium price as 'gourmet' courgettes. If 2% of his crop attracts this premium, calculate the standard deviation for his courgette weights.

b The largest courgettes return a much lower price because they are classified as marrows. If 5% of his crop consists of marrows, calculate the minimum weight for a courgette to be classified as a marrow.

8 Anna skateboards to school. On average it takes her 6 minutes and 32 seconds, with a standard deviation of 53 seconds. Her brother Mike rides his bike and he takes 5 minutes and 41 seconds, with a standard deviation of 26 seconds. School starts at 8.30 a.m.

a If they both leave home at 8.25 a.m., who is more likely to be late? Support your answer with calculations.

b If both must leave home at the same time, calculate the time that they must leave if both are to arrive at school in time on 95% of days.

ISBN: 9780170354240

3 Mixed normal distribution problems

1 An investigation was carried out into the length of time that different light bulbs last. It was found that Bargain Bulbs lasted on average 4500 hours, with a standard deviation of 350 hours, and that the lengths of time they lasted was normally distributed.

a Calculate the probability that a Bargain Bulb will last between 4500 and 5000 hours.

b Calculate the probability that a Bargain Bulb lasts less than 3500 hours.

It has been found that 98% of energy-saver light bulbs lasts between 6000 and 15,000 hours. If the lifespan of these bulbs is normally distributed:

c Calculate the mean of this distribution.

d Calculate its standard deviation.

e The company director would like 98% of light bulbs to last longer than 7000 hours. If the standard deviation remains the same, what would the new mean length of life span need to be?

ISBN: 9780170354240

2 A forest of pine trees has heights that are normally distributed with a mean of 28 m and a standard deviation of 1.5 m.

a Calculate the probability that a tree is between 26 m and 28 m high.

b Calculate the probability that a tree is less than 31 m high.

c If the forest contains 120,000 tress, how many would be expected to be more than 31 m high?

Two species of pine are growing together in a forest. Species A has a mean height of 32 m with a standard deviation of 2.3 m. Species B has a mean height of 30 m with a standard deviation of 1.2 m. The tree heights are normally distributed. The forester plans to mill the trees when they reach 28 m.

d Which species has a greater percentage of trees that are too small to be milled? Support your answer with calculations.

e The forester would like to adjust his minimum height for milling so that he harvests exactly the same proportion of each species. Calculate the minimum height and the proportion of trees that are big enough to mill.

ISBN: 9780170354240

Probability trees

There is a special team's award presented at a school assembly, and the hockey team has been chosen to receive the award. The award must be accepted by the captain or, if the captain is absent, the vice-captain. The captain of the hockey team is present in assembly 95% of the time. The vice-captain is present in assembly 93% of the time that the captain is present, and 75% of the time when the captain is absent.

a Calculate the probability that both the captain and the vice-captain are present in this assembly.
b Calculate the probability that the award will be presented in this assembly.

Steps:

1 Decide what the **events** are, and their order:
Event 1 will be that the captain is in the assembly.
Event 2 will be that the vice-captain is in the assembly.
Write the **events** at the **ends** of the branches.

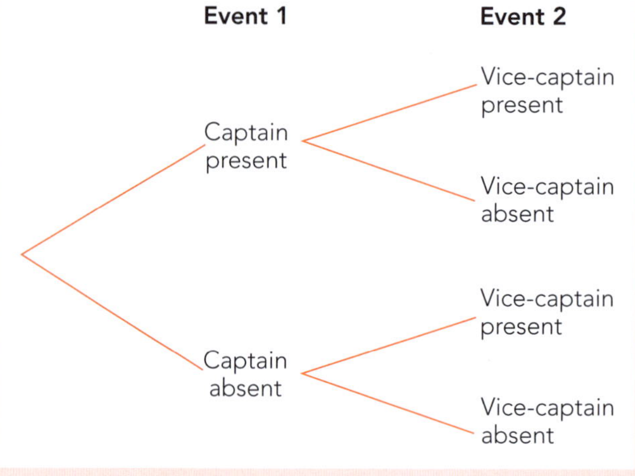

2 Add the **probabilities** of each event to the **middle** of each branch:

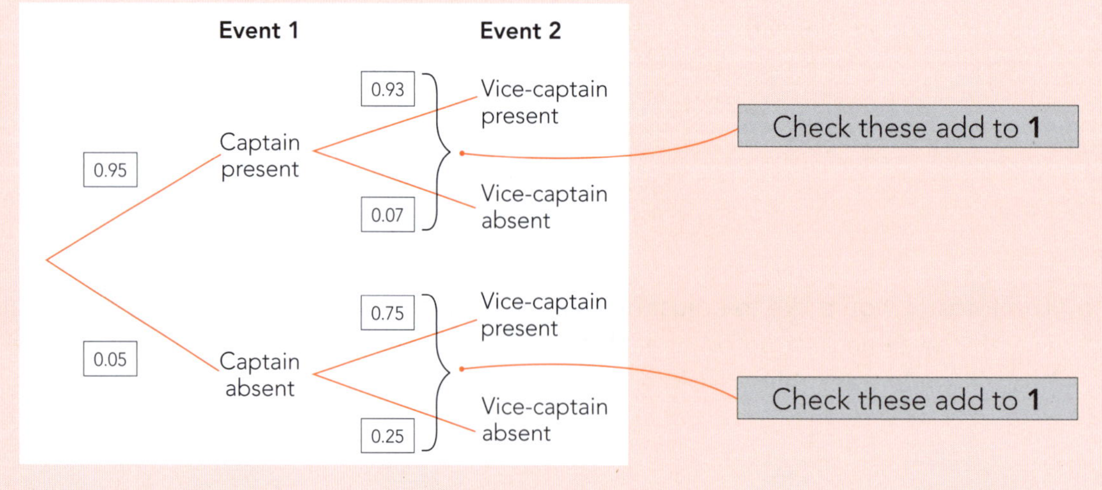

ISBN: 9780170354240

3 **Check** that the probabilities for every branch add to **1**.

4 **List** the outcomes at the ends of each branch, and calculate the probabilities at each end. You **multiply** the probabilities along each branch because Event 1 **and** Event 2 must occur.

(Note: C′ means not the captain and V′ means not the vice-captain.)

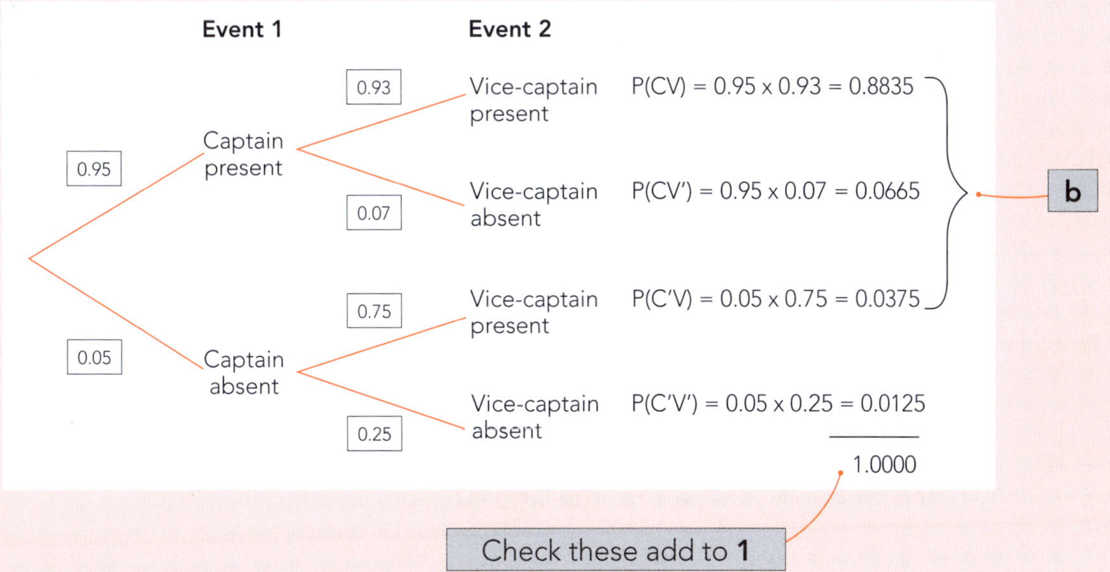

Check these add to **1**

5 **Check** that your probabilities in the right-hand column **add** to **1**. The reason is that one of CV **or** CV′ **or** C′V **or** C′V′ **must** occur.

6 Highlight the events required, along with their probabilities.
Add these to find the overall probability required.

Answers:

a P(captain and vice-captain present) = 0.8835

b P(either one or both of them is present) = 0.8835 + 0.0665 + 0.0375 = 0.9875

ISBN: 9780170354240

Use probability trees to answer the following questions.

1 A teacher is marking a very large number of test papers. Of those sitting the test, 55% are boys, and the probability that a boy passes the test is 0.6. The probability that a girl passes the test is 0.7.

a Complete the probability tree.

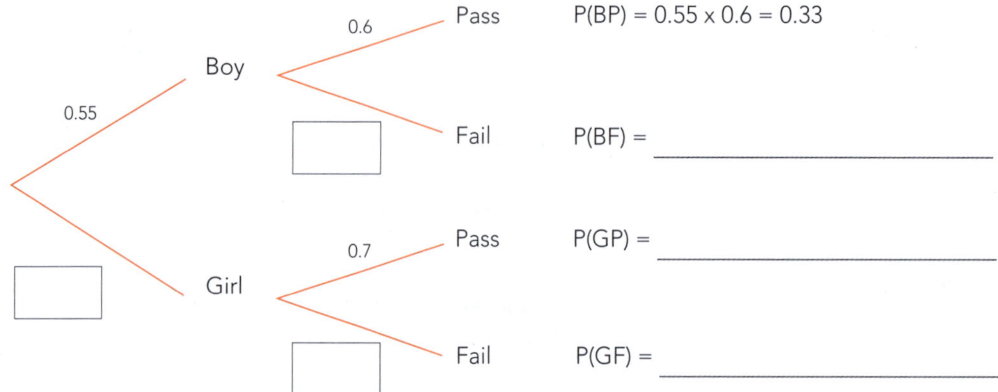

b Calculate the probability that a paper belongs to a boy who fails the test.

c Calculate the probability that a paper belongs to a girl who fails the test.

d Calculate the probability that a paper belongs to a boy.

e Calculate the probability that a paper belongs to a student who has failed the test.

f If 1600 students sat the test, how many failed it? (Use your answer from **e**.)

g Calculate the probability that a paper belongs to either a girl or a student who has failed the test.

h Calculate the probability that a paper belongs to a boy who has passed the test. Compare this answer to your previous one. Explain.

ISBN: 9780170354240

2 Wiremu walks to school on 70% of school days, and bikes on the rest. If he walks, then the probability that he has time to make his lunch is 0.4, otherwise he has to buy it. When he bikes to school, he makes his lunch 80% of the time.

a Complete the probability tree.

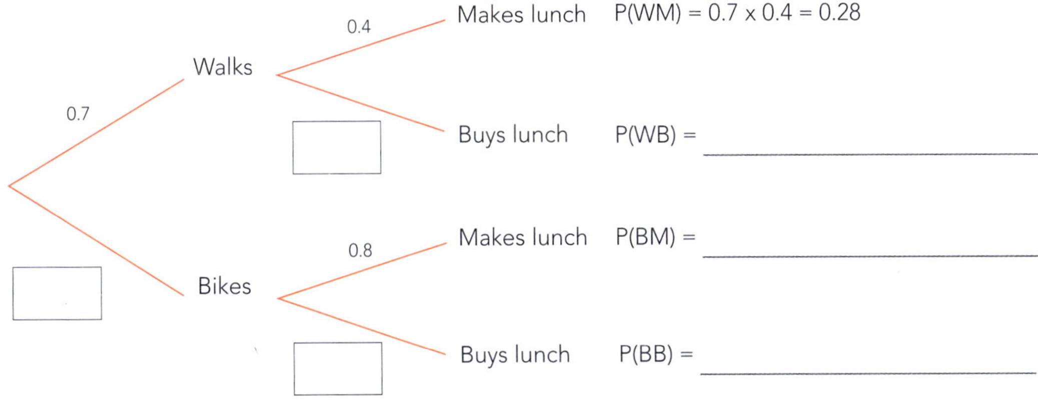

b Calculate the probability that on a particular day, Wiremu walks to school and buys his lunch.

c Calculate the probability that on a particular day, Wiremu bikes to school and makes his lunch.

d Calculate the probability that on a particular day, Wiremu buys his lunch.

e If there are 48 days in the term, on about how many days will Wiremu buy his lunch?

f Calculate the probability that on a particular day, Wiremu either walks or buys his lunch.

g If he has made his lunch, what is the probability that he has biked to school?

h Calculate the proportion of days that he walks to school, given that he buys his lunch.

ISBN: 9780170354240

3 A policeman is checking cars at a road block for registration and warrants of fitness. He finds that 7% of cars are unregistered. If a car is unregistered, then there is a 23% chance that it will have no warrant of fitness. If a car is registered, there is a 5% chance it has no warrant of fitness. Record this information on the following tree diagram.

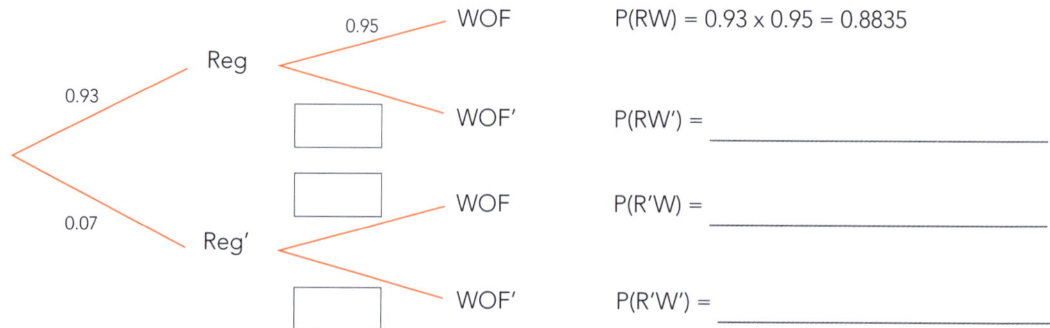

a Calculate the percentage of cars that are not registered and have no warrant of fitness.

b If he checked 500 cars in a week, how many cars would he expect to find with neither registration nor a warrant of fitness?

c Calculate the percentage of cars that are either registered or have a warrant of fitness.

d Calculate the percentage of unregistered cars that have no warrant of fitness.

e Calculate the percentage of unwarranted cars that are not registered.

4 Rebekah tosses three coins. The probability tree shows the possible outcomes. Complete the probability tree.

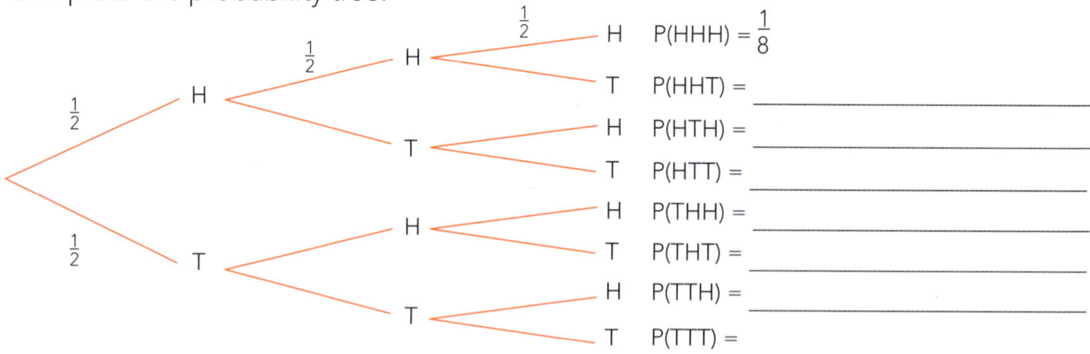

a Calculate the probability of getting one or more heads.

b Calculate the probability of getting exactly two tails.

c If she got exactly two tails, calculate the probability that she got them in the first two tosses.

ISBN: 9780170354240

5 Hari proposes a game in which three dice are rolled. If two of them are 6, then you win a point. Complete the probability tree.

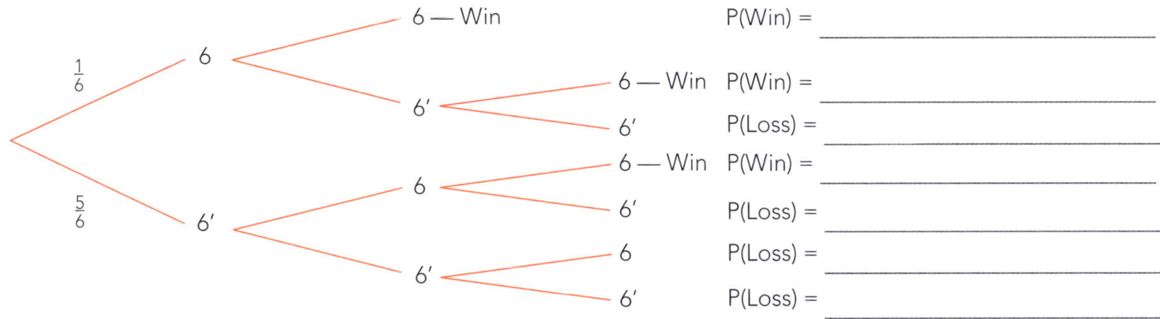

a Calculate the probability of a win.

b If Hari wins, what is the probability that he won in three rolls?

6 A husband and wife are offered the opportunity to bungy jump. The probability that the wife jumps is 0.7. If the wife decides to jump, then the probability that her husband also jumps is 0.8. If the woman doesn't jump, then the probability that her husband jumps is 0.6. Draw a probability tree to illustrate this situation.

a Calculate the probability that neither bungy jumps.

b Calculate the probability that just one of them jumps.

c Given that just one of them jumps, calculate the probability that it was the husband.

ISBN: 9780170354240

7 Grandma has lollies in a jar. There are 10 mints, 6 fruit drops and 4 caramels. Emma is allowed one after lunch and one after dinner. Complete the following probability tree.

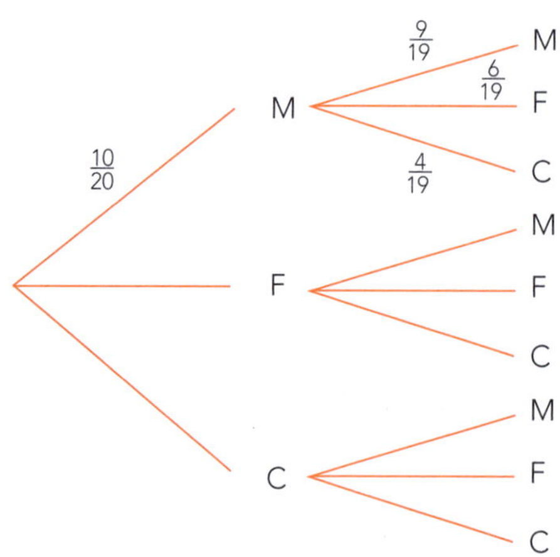

a Calculate the probability that she got two caramels.

b Calculate the probability that she got two different lollies.

c If her two lollies were the same, calculate the probability that they were both mints.

d If Emma was allowed to take three lollies, calculate the probability that all three were mints.

e Calculate the probability that all three were the same.

f The following week, Grandma once again had 20 lollies in her jar, but with different numbers of each type. If the probability of getting two fruit drops was $\frac{42}{380}$, how many fruit drops were in the jar at the start?

g The week after that, Grandma had 24 lollies in the jar, and the probability of getting two fruit drops was $\frac{7}{69}$. How many fruit drops were in the jar at the start?

 ISBN: 9780170354240

8 An arborist who works for the city council has discovered that 59% of protected trees in the city are diseased. If they are diseased, then the probability that they will need to be felled within the next 10 years is 0.95. The probability a tree is healthy **and** felled in the next 10 years is 0.123. In the space below, draw a probability tree for this.

a Calculate the probability that a randomly chosen protected tree in the city will need to be felled in the next 10 years.

b If a tree has to be felled, what is the probability that it is diseased?

c If 1094 trees had to be felled over the 10-year period, estimate (to the nearest 10) the total number of protected trees in the city.

9 Alex is playing Bianca at chess. The first person to win two games will be declared the overall winner. The probability that Alex wins the first game is 0.6. If he won the previous game, then the probability that he wins the next game is 0.65. If he lost the previous game, then the probability of winning the next game is 0.55. They stop playing when one of them has won a total of two games. Draw a probability tree showing this.

a Calculate the probability that they finish after just two games.

b Calculate the probability that Alex is the overall winner.

c If Alex is the overall winner, what is the probability that three games were played?

ISBN: 9780170354240

10 At Wildbank Animal Park, some of the deer have contracted daffy deer disease. There is a test for this, but it is not 100% reliable. If a deer has the disease, it will test positive 95% of the time. If the deer does not have the disease, it will to test negative 90% of the time (that is, 10% of those that don't have the disease will give a positive result). It is known that 20% of this population has the disease. Draw a probability tree to show this.

a What is the probability that an individual in this population tests positive for this disease?

b What proportion of those that test positive actually have the disease?

c How would the proportion in **b** change if only 10% of the population actually had the disease?

11 Four cards are drawn from a normal 52-card pack. Sketch probability trees to help do the following calculations, remembering that there are only two branches at each stage.

a Calculate the probability that all are black.

b Calculate the probability that all are aces.

c Calculate the probability of drawing three aces and then a king.

d Calculate the probability of drawing two hearts and then two spades.

e Calculate the probability of drawing a spade, then a club, then a diamond and then a heart.

f Calculate the probability of drawing two red cards, followed by a spade and a club in either order.

  ISBN: 9780170354240

Probability tables

- These can be used for frequencies, percentages, probabilities or fractions.
- You may be given some or all of the table, or you might have to create one from given information.
- They are sometimes an alternative to probability trees.

Tables of frequencies

Example: The following table shows the numbers of girls and boys from Years 12 and 13 who are going to the school ball.

	Year 12	Year 13	Total
Girls	47		
Boys		48	
Total		97	185

a Complete the table. The steps are shown in a clockwise direction.

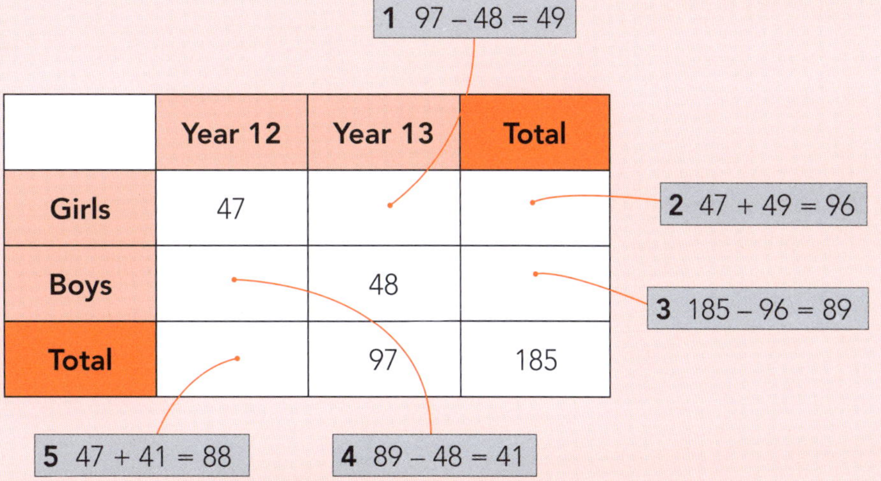

	Year 12	Year 13	Total
Girls	47		
Boys		48	
Total		97	185

Now CHECK that all the rows and columns add up correctly!

b Calculate the percentage of those attending the formal who are Year 13 girls.

$$\text{Percentage who are Year 13 girls} = \frac{49}{185} \times 100 = 26.5\%$$

ISBN: 9780170354240

Try this question:

In Auckland, a trial spot check by the police for registration and warrants of fitness of 500 cars revealed the following data. Complete the table.

	Registered	Unregistered	Total
WOF		22	
No WOF			92
Total	454		500

a Calculate the proportion of cars that was unregistered.

b Calculate the probability that a car has no warrant of fitness.

c Calculate the probability that an unregistered car has no warrant of fitness.

d What conclusion can you draw from your answers to the last two questions?

e Calculate the probability that a car checked in this trial either had no warrant of fitness or was unregistered.

f The police would like to extend these spot checks to cover 10,000 cars from all around the country. Based on the previous data, how many unregistered cars are they likely to find? State any assumptions you have made in calculating your answer.

g When the police carry out this extended check, it is proposed that children in the registered cars which also have a warrant of fitness are to be given a lollipop. If the average number of children in each car is 1.15, estimate the number of lollipops that the police will need.

  ISBN: 9780170354240

Creating your own table

Example: The 280 Year 12 students at Academia High School must study either English or Te Reo. Nobody studies both. All but 13 of the 82 who study Te Reo are in the kapa haka group. There are 97 in the kapa haka group. Complete the table below.

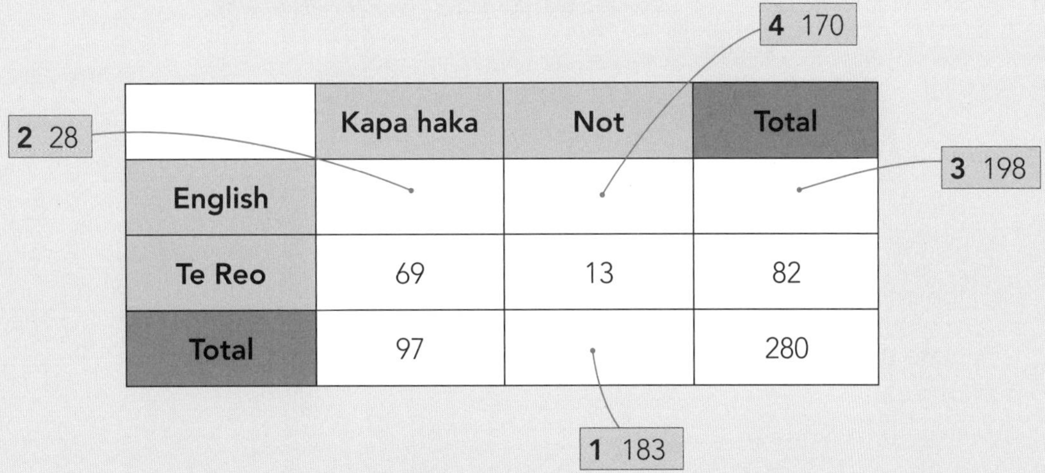

	Kapa haka	Not	Total
English			
Te Reo	69	13	82
Total	97		280

a Calculate the percentage of those studying English who are in the kapa haka group.

$$\text{Percentage in kapa haka} = \frac{28}{198} \times 100 = 14.1\%$$

b What proportion of students who study Te Reo is in the kapa haka group?

$$\text{Proportion of students in the kapa haka group} = \frac{69}{82} = 0.8415$$

c Calculate the probability that a randomly selected student at Academia High School either is in the kapa haka group or studies Te Reo.

(Note: The NZQA interpretation of 'either' is one or the other **or both**.)

$$\text{Probability that student does either} = \frac{97 + 13}{280} = 0.3929 \left(\text{or } \frac{280 - 170}{280}\right)$$

d A headline in an education publication states 'Students who do kapa haka are 10 times more likely to study Te Reo than those who don't'.

State whether or not you agree with this headline, and support your answer with full reasons and calculations.

$$\text{P(studies Te Reo given that is in kapa haka)} = \frac{69}{97} = 0.7113$$

$$\text{P(studies Te Reo given that is not in kapa haka)} = \frac{13}{183} = 0.0710$$

I agree with the headline because 10 x 0.0710 is very close to 0.7113.

ISBN: 9780170354240

Try this question:

An analysis was done of sports participation at Olympic High School. Of the 1200 students, 65% play sport. Girls make up 52% of the school roll, and 360 girls play sport.

	Girls	Boys	Total
Sport			
No sport			
Total			

a Use the information given to complete the table.

b Calculate the probability that a randomly selected girl from Olympic High School plays sport.

c Calculate the probability that a randomly chosen sports player from Olympic High School is a girl.

d Calculate the percentage of boys who do not play sport.

e Calculate the probability that a randomly selected student from Olympic High School is either a boy or a sports player.

f The principal has funds to encourage more sports participation. Would you recommend that he targets boys or girls with the funding? Give statistical justifications for your answer.

g A headline in the school newsletter says 'Boys are 30% more likely to play sport than girls'. Investigate whether this headline is justified or not.

ISBN: 9780170354240

Tables of probabilities

Example: The percentages of male and female staff and students at Academia High School are given below. Complete the table.

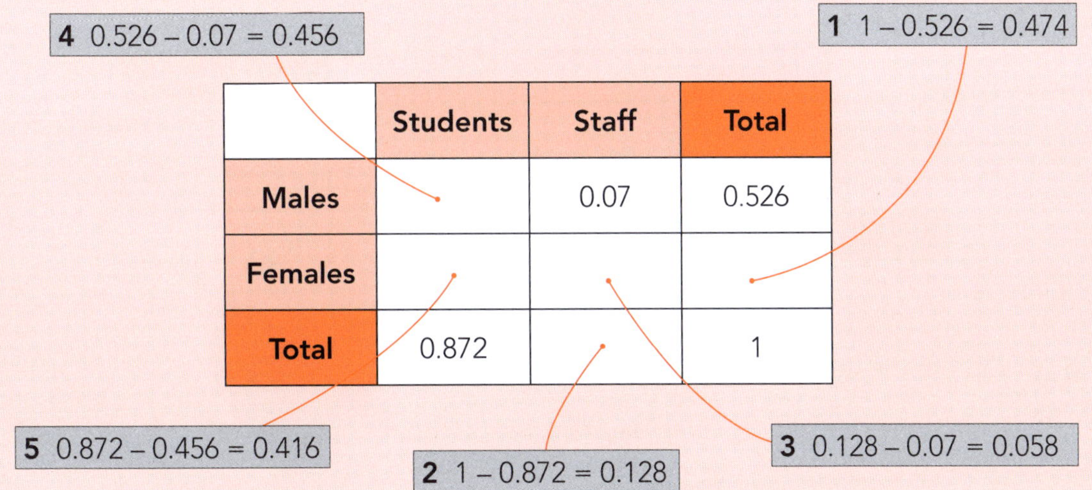

	Students	Staff	Total
Males		0.07	0.526
Females			
Total	0.872		1

a If there are 1308 students at Academia High School, calculate the total number of people who study or teach there.

$$0.872 \times \text{total number} = 1308$$
$$\text{Total number} = 1308/0.872 = 1500$$

b How many male students attend the school?

$$\text{Number of male students} = 0.456 \times 1500 = 684$$

c What percentage of the staff is male?

$$\text{Percentage of staff that is male} = \frac{0.07}{0.128} \times 100 = 54.7\%$$

d Calculate the proportion of females that are students.

$$\text{Proportion of females that are students} = \frac{0.416}{0.474} = 0.878$$

e Calculate the probability that a randomly chosen student is female.

$$\text{Probability that a student is female} = \frac{0.416}{0.872} = 0.477$$

ISBN: 9780170354240

Try this question:

A new track has been built for use by those on mountain bikes or on foot. The council has analysed a survey of all track users in which they were asked whether they used it on foot or on mountain bikes. The probability that a track user was a male was 0.52. The probability that a track user was a male who walked was 0.21, and a female who walked was 0.34.

	Bike	Foot	Total
Males			
Females			
Total			1

a Complete the table.

b Calculate the proportion of female track users who mountain-biked it.

c Calculate the proportion of mountain bikers who were females.

d If there were 585 mountain bikers who did the survey, calculate the total number of track users who did it.

e Calculate the number of track users who were either female or on foot.

f It is estimated that a mountain biker does about twice the damage to the track compared with a person on foot. Estimate the total proportion of damage to the track done by mountain bikers.

g The head ranger for the track told his boss that females were twice as likely as males to walk the track. Was this true? Justify your answer.

 ISBN: 9780170354240

Use tables to solve the following problems.

1 Anna attends a country school where only 25% of students arrive at school other than by school bus; the school roll is made up of three boys to every two girls; and 50% of the students are boys who arrive by bus.

a Complete the following table.

	Girls	Boys	Total
Bus			
Other			
Total			100%

b What proportion of girls arrives at school by bus?

c What proportion of students arrives at school by bus?

d What do the answers to **b** and **c** tell you about the proportion of boys who bus to school?

e Calculate the probability that a randomly chosen student is either a girl or travels to school by bus.

f If the school roll is 560, how many girls come to school by means other than by bus?

g Over the holidays, three families move into the school zone, and all of their children need to catch the bus to school. Between them they have eight girls and two boys. Complete the table below to show the numbers of students in each category.

	Girls	Boys	Total
Bus			
Other			
Total			570

ISBN: 9780170354240

2 A restaurant offers a dinner deal in which patrons can choose soup or mussels as a starter, followed by steak, fish or a vegetarian dish as a main. The table below shows the numbers of people making each choice during one weekend. Everybody ate a starter and a main course.

	Steak	Fish	Vegetarian	Totals
Soup	63	65	52	180
Mussels	31	67	19	117
Totals	94	132	71	297

a Calculate the probability that a patron ate soup.

b Calculate the probability that a patron ate soup and fish.

c Calculate the percentage of people who ate mussels or fish.

d Calculate the proportion of steak eaters who selected mussels as a starter.

e Calculate the proportion of those who chose the fish who had mussels to start with.

f Write a sentence comparing your last two answers.

g Calculate the proportion of patrons who ate no seafood in their meal.

h A car rally is being held in the town during the following weekend. The chef estimates that they will sell about 400 meals. Estimate the number of steaks that he should order.

ISBN: 9780170354240

Risk

- The word 'risk' refers to the probability of something bad happening. Nobody ever talks about the risk of winning Lotto. However, the risks of car crashes or catching a disease are commonly discussed.
- The term 'likelihood ratio' is sometimes used insead of 'risk'.
- **There are two types of risk that you need to be able to calculate: absolute risk and relative risk.**

Absolute risk

This is simply the probability of something (bad) happening.

Example: A group of 5000 patients who suffered from a skin condition was split into two groups of 2500. Those in one group were given a new drug, and of these, 399 reported itching as a side effect. Those in the second group were given a placebo, and of these, 42 reported itching.

Group given drug: Absolute risk of itching $= \frac{399}{2500} = 0.1596$

Group given placebo: Absolute risk of itching $= \frac{42}{2500} = 0.0168$

Relative risk

This is the risk of one event divided by the risk of a second event.

$$\text{Relative risk} = \frac{\text{Absolute risk of event A}}{\text{Absolute risk of event B}}$$

Relative risk > 1 ⟶ The risk is greater for event A than for event B.

Example:

Relative risk of itching with the drug compared with the placebo $= \frac{0.1596}{0.0168} = 9.5$

This means that patients given the drug are 9.5 times **as** likely to experience itching than those given the placebo.

Relative risk = 1 ⟶ The risk is the same for both events.

Relative risk < 1 ⟶ The risk is less for event A than event B.

Example:

Relative risk of itching with the placebo compared with the drug $= \frac{0.0168}{0.1596} = 0.105$

This means that patients given the placebo are 0.105 times **as** likely to experience itching as those given the drug.

ISBN: 9780170354240

Risk and tables

Risk and relative risk can also be calculated from tables.

Example: For a term, Wiremu keeps a record of whether he walks or bikes to school, and whether he is late. His results are shown in the table.

	Not late	Late	Total
Bike	24	4	28
Walk	12	10	22
Total	36	14	50

a Calculate the absolute risk that Wiremu is late to school.

$$\text{Absolute risk of being late} = \frac{\text{Total number of times he is late}}{\text{Total number of days in term}} = \frac{14}{50} = 0.28$$

b Calculate the probability that he is late on a day when he walks to school.

$$\text{Probability} = \frac{\text{Number of times he was late if he walked}}{\text{Number of times he walked}} = \frac{10}{22} = 0.4545$$

c Calculate the probability that he is late on a day when he bikes to school.

$$\text{Probability} = \frac{\text{Number of times he was late if he biked}}{\text{Number of times he biked}} = \frac{4}{28} = 0.1429$$

d Calculate the relative risk of being late when he walks to school compared with when he bikes.

$$\text{Relative risk} = \frac{\text{Probability of being late if he walks}}{\text{Probability of being late if he biked}} = \frac{0.4545}{0.1429} = 3.18$$

e Explain what your result means.

Wiremu is more than three times as likely to be late if he walks to school compared with if he bikes. So if he wants to get to school on time, he should go on his bike.

ISBN: 9780170354240

Use tables to solve the following problems.

1 For one term, Mere kept a record of how she travelled to school and whether or not she was late. She walked on 30 out of the 55 days. She was late on a total of 32 days, and of these, 21 were when she walked.

a Complete the following table using the information given.

	Late	On time	Total
Walk			
Bus			
Total			

b Calculate the absolute risk of being late to school.

c Calculate the probability that she is late on a day when she walks to school.

d Calculate the probability that she is late on a day when she catches the bus to school.

e Calculate the relative risk of being late when she walks to school compared with when she catches the bus.

f Explain what this means.

ISBN: 9780170354240

2 One thousand students were divided into two groups. Those in the first group drank three standard alcoholic drinks each. Those in the second group drank three standard non-alcoholic drinks. They were then given a standardised coordination test. These results are shown below.

	Pass	Fail	Total
Three standard alcoholic drinks	438	162	600
Three standard non-alcoholic drinks	340	60	400
Total	778	222	1000

a Calculate the absolute risk of failing the coordination test.

b Calculate the absolute risk of failing the test after three alcoholic drinks.

c Calculate the absolute risk of failing the test after three non-alcoholic drinks.

d Calculate the relative risk of failing the coordination test for students who drank three alcoholic drinks compared with those who had non-alcoholic drinks.

e Explain the meaning of your previous answer.

f A different group of 60 students was given three non-alcoholic drinks, followed by the same coordination test. How many would you expect to pass the test? Would you be surprised if 53 passed the test? Why?

ISBN: 9780170354240

3 During the winter term 35% of students at a school caught a cold. Of these, 40% took days off. Only 10% of those who didn't catch the cold took days off during the term.

a Use the information to complete the table

	Cold	No cold	Total
Days off	0.14		
No days off			
Total			

b Calculate the absolute risk of catching a cold.

c Calculate the absolute risk of taking days off for those who caught a cold.

d Calculate the absolute risk of taking days off for those who didn't catch a cold.

e Calculate the relative risk of taking days off for those who caught a cold compared with those who didn't catch a cold.

f Explain what this means.

g Calculate the relative risk of catching a cold for those who didn't take days off compared with those who did take days off.

h Explain what this means.

ISBN: 9780170354240

4 A study of 10,000 people aged 66 years or older was completed. Of these, 15% was diabetic. Of those who were diabetic, 12 had fractured their hips. However, 55 of those who were not diabetic had fractured their hips.

a Complete the table.

	Hip fracture	No hip fracture	Total
Diabetes			
No diabetes			
Total			

b Calculate the risk of being a diabetic and fracturing a hip within a given year for those aged 66 or older.

c Calculate the probability that a person with diabetes fractures a hip.

d Calculate the probability that a person without diabetes fractures a hip.

e Calculate the relative risk of hip fracture for those with diabetes compared with those without diabetes.

f Explain what your answer means.

g Calculate the relative risk of diabetes for those who fracture their hips compared with those who don't fracture their hips.

h Explain what your answer means.

ISBN: 9780170354240

5 Data from two groups of three to six year olds were analysed to see if there is a relationship between drinking soft drinks between meals and tooth extraction due to decay.

	Soft drinks between meals	No soft drinks between meals	Total
One or more molar extracted	45	12	57
No molars extracted	455	488	943
Total	500	500	1000

a Calculate the absolute risk of having one or more molars extracted for the group who never drank soft drinks between meals.

b Calculate the absolute risk of having one or more molars extracted for the group who drank soft drinks between meals.

c Calculate the relative risk to molars of drinking soft drinks between meals compared with not drinking them.

d Explain what your previous answer means.

6 Flying is often seen as risky. The population of a European country was approximately 58,858,000. The number of people killed in road traffic accidents was 1612. The number of people killed as passengers on an airline was 17.

a Calculate the absolute risk of being killed in a road traffic accident.

b Calculate the absolute risk of being killed as a passenger on an airline.

c Show that a person from this country is about 95 times more likely to be killed in a road traffic accident compared with being killed as a passenger on an airline.

ISBN: 9780170354240

7 Tests for medical conditions are not usually 100% accurate. A certain form of cancer affects one in 10,000 people. The test for it gives a true positive result in 98% of cases, and a true negative result in 99% of cases.

a Show that the risk of having this form of cancer if you tested positive is approximately one in 100.

b Show that if you test negative for this condition, it is almost certain that you do not have it.

8 The absolute risk of catching a particular disease is five in 100. A company develops a drug which it maintains will reduce the absolute risk of catching the disease by 20%. Calculate the absolute risk of catching the disease for those who take the drug.

9 The absolute risk of developing a form of cancer is 0.0004. An adviser claims that the absolute risk of developing this form of cancer is reduced by 25% if a particular diet is followed.

a Calculate the absolute risk of developing this form of cancer if the diet is followed.

b On average, how many people per 10,000 would avoid developing this form of cancer by following this diet?

  ISBN: 9780170354240

Practice questions

Practice question one

Two types of cats live on an island. There are domestic (household) cats and feral cats (domestic cats that have gone wild). The feral cats are a major threat to wildlife.
All the 28 domestic cats were listed and weighed.

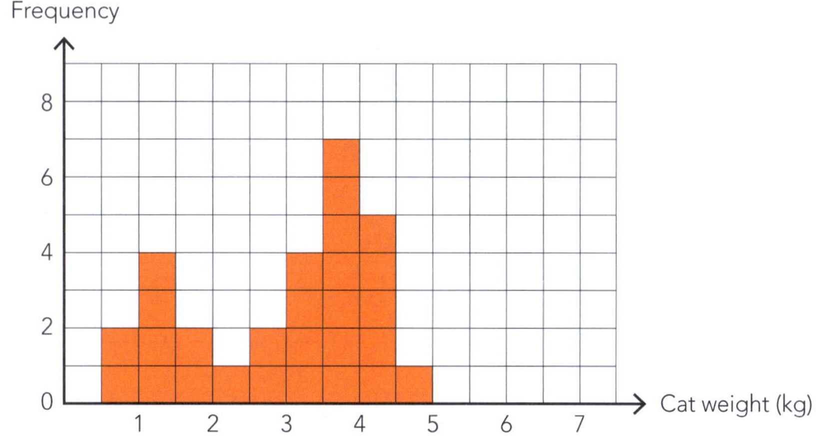

a Calculate the probability that a domestic cat weighs less than 2 kg.

b The weights of feral cats on the island are normally distributed with a mean weight of 4.1 kg and a standard deviation of 0.8 kg. On the axis below, sketch this distribution.

c One hundred and twenty-two feral cats are trapped. Calculate the number of these that would be expected to weigh between 4.1 kg and 5 kg.

ISBN: 9780170354240

d Martin traps two cats in one day. Calculate the probability that both weigh between 4.1 kg and 5 kg.

e It is estimated that there are 3500 feral cats on the island. Cats that weigh more than 6 kg are of great concern because they are too big to fit into traps. Calculate the number of feral cats that are likely to be over 6 kg.

f Martin would like to display the distribution of the weights of feral cats on a box plot. Calculate the upper and lower quartiles.

g Compare and contrast the distributions of domestic and feral cats. You should discuss shape, centre and spread in relation to the context.

  ISBN: 9780170354240

Practice question two

Influenza vaccinations are offered to all students in a school. Of the 950 students, 327 take up the offer and are vaccinated. A total of 193 students catch the flu during the following winter, and of these, 21 were vaccinated.

You may complete the table below to help you answer the questions.

	Influenza	No influenza	Total
Vaccinated			
Unvaccinated			
Total			

a Calculate the probability that a vaccinated student got the flu.

b What proportion of the unvaccinated students got the flu?

c Calculate the relative risk of catching the flu for unvaccinated students compared with vaccinated students. Explain what your answer means.

d A similar school with a roll of 2976 is considering offering influenza vaccinations. Based on the experience of the smaller school, how many cases of influenza are likely to be prevented by vaccination? Show your reasoning. State any assumptions that you made in your calculations.

ISBN: 9780170354240

Members of the local croquet club are offered influenza vaccinations. Experience has shown that for those who have the vaccination, the probability that they will get the flu is two in 100. About 15% of those who choose not to have the vaccination are likely to get the 'flu. Of the 95 club members, 76 decide to have the vaccination.

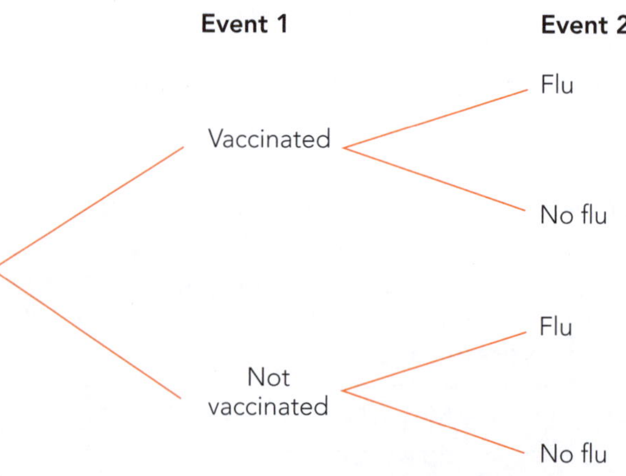

e Use the probability tree to help you to calculate the probability that a club member was unvaccinated and got the flu.

f Estimate the number of club members who got the flu. Show your calculations.

g Calculate the relative risk of getting the flu for those who were not vaccinated compared with those who were. Explain what this means.

ISBN: 9780170354240

Practice question three

A disease is discovered that affects one dairy cow in every 100. Rather than treat entire herds with a costly drug, it is more economic to test each cow for the disease. However, the test for this disease is not completely accurate: 90% of those who have the disease will produce a positive result, and for those that do not have the disease, the test is 99% accurate. Use the probability tree below to help you with the questions.

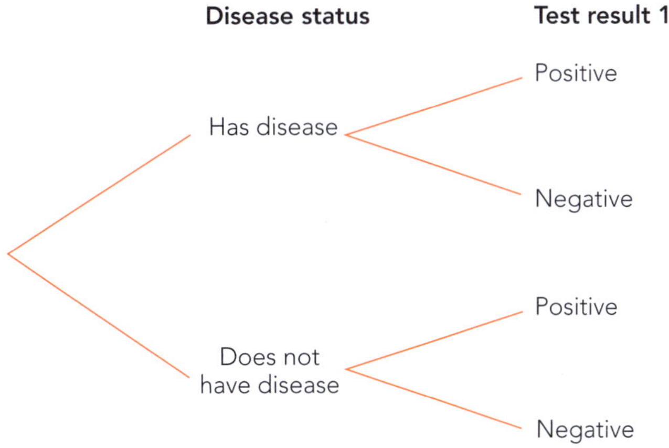

a Calculate the probability that a cow returns a positive test for this disease.

b If a cow returned a positive test, calculate the probability that it has this disease.

c Ten thousand dairy cows were tested for the disease. How many cows would be expected to return a negative test even though they actually had the disease?

ISBN: 9780170354240

d A veterinary surgeon has calculated that for all the cows that returned positive tests, the relative risk of having the disease compared with not having it is 10 out of 11. Use calculations to show that she is correct.

Unfortunately, the cost for treatment of this disease increases dramatically. If the results of just the first test are used, then only 10 cows in every 21 treated actually have the disease. Therefore a second test is given to all the cows that returned a positive result in the first test. This second test is 95% accurate, whether or not the cow has the disease. You may wish to add to the probability tree in order to help you with these questions.

e For all the cows who returned two positive tests, calculate the relative risk of having the disease compared with not having it.

f For a herd of 900 cows, estimate the number of cows that would need to be treated because they returned two positive tests. Show your calculations.

ISBN: 9780170354240

Answers

Probabilities are rounded to a maximum of 4 dp.
Z values are rounded to a maximum of 3 dp.
Normal distribution answers have been done using tables.
Where a graphics calculator answer differs from the tables answer, this is indicated next to the letters GC.
Professional judgement should apply.

Probability revision (p. 7)

1 ✘ It's not possible to have probabilities that are bigger than 1.
2 ✘ He should have marked it correct because probabilities can be either fractions or decimals, and $0.5 = \frac{1}{2}$
3 ✘ Should be $\frac{\text{Number who own a cat}}{\text{Number in the class}} = \frac{25}{28}$
4 ✓ $\frac{1}{4}$ of 28 = 7. However, this is only the expected number. It is quite likely to be more or fewer than 7.
5 ✘ $P(\text{odd}) = \frac{1}{2}$, $P(10) = \frac{1}{10}$
Correct answer: $P(\text{odd or } 10) = \frac{1}{2} + \frac{1}{10} = \frac{6}{10} = \frac{3}{5}$
Incorrect answer: $P(\text{odd or } 10) = \frac{1}{2} \times \frac{1}{10} = \frac{1}{20}$
6 ✓ $P(10 \text{ and } 10) = \frac{1}{10} \times \frac{1}{10} = \frac{1}{100} = 0.01$
7 ✘ Not possible to have negative probabilities.
8 ✓ $P(2) = \frac{1}{6}$, $P(2) = \frac{1}{6}$. So $P(2 \text{ or } 3) = \frac{1}{6} + \frac{1}{6} = \frac{1}{3}$

Graphs of distributions (pp. 8–15)

pp. 11–15

1 a $\frac{22}{100} = 0.22$
b $\frac{3}{13} = 0.2308$. These values are close, but you would not expect to get this value exactly when drawing only 100 cards, due to chance.
c $\frac{13}{100}$
d All the cards were drawn about eight times, but Jacks were drawn only six times, and 2s were drawn 10 times. The distribution is roughly rectangular and symmetrical.
e I would expect a more even distribution and it should look more rectangular, with most cards being drawn $\frac{1000}{13}$ = about 77 times.

2 a $\frac{16}{60} = 26.67\%$
b $\frac{23}{60} = 0.3833$
c Cars had between 0 and 10 faults, with a range of 10. The most common number of faults was 0 (16 cars), but the frequency dropped as the number of faults increased, so the distribution is very skewed to the right and therefore not symmetrical.

3 a $\frac{1}{69} = 1.45\%$
b 3 faults
c The number of faults for the two companies were between similar values (0–10 and 0–8), so the ranges were similar (10 and 8). However, the modes were very different: 0 faults for Happy Hire and 3 faults for Rogue Rentals, so Happy Hire cars were more reliable. The shapes of the distributions were very different, with Happy Hire being very skewed to the right, so most cars had few faults, compared with the roughly normal distribution for Rogue Rentals, where most cars had between 2 and 5 faults.

4 a $\frac{6}{40} = 0.15$
b $\frac{26}{40} = 0.65$
c Heights between 142 cm and 164 cm.
Range = 22 cm. Most common height is 152–154 cm.
Shape — similar to a normal distribution.
Symmetry — almost symmetrical.
d Only 15% of Year 7s were over 158 cm, whereas 75% of Year 8s were over 158 cm.

5 a $\frac{5}{65} = 7.69\%$
b $\frac{30}{65} = 0.4615$
c Birds' weights between 1.9 kg and 4.0 kg. Range of weights is 2.1 kg. Most common weights are 2.3–2.4 kg and 2.7–2.8 kg. Shape is bimodal, and it is not symmetrical, but skewed to the right due to three particularly heavy birds.

6 a $\frac{11}{40} = 0.2750$
b Amounts between \$0 and \$130. Range \$130. Most spent between \$50 and \$60. Irregular shape and not symmetrical.

7 a New Zealand novels over this period had between 150 and 550 pages, apart from one which had 800–850 pages. The range of pages for the novels, apart from the very long one, was 400 pages. The most common length is 300–350 pages, but most having between 330 and 450 pages. The distribution is roughly normal and symmetrical.
b 11.84%
c Between 300 and 350 pages.

The normal distribution (pp. 16–53)

The standard normal distribution (p. 18)

1	a 2	b -1.33	
2	a 0	b 2.5	c -3
3	a 2.045	b -4.091	
4	a -0.286	b 2.571	
5	a -5	b 3.091	

1 Calculating probabilites (pp. 19–37)

Reading normal distribution tables (p. 21)

1	0.4032	2	0.4970	3	0.4750
4	0.45	5	0.4994	6	0.2512
7	0.4787	8	0.5	9	0.4975
10	0.0032				

Calculating a probability on the right side of the curve (p. 22)

1 $Z = 2$, $P = 0.4772$ 2 $Z = 1.692$, $P = 0.4547$
3 $Z = 1.818$, $P = 0.4655$

Probabilities below a value (p. 23)

$Z = 2 \rightarrow P = 0.9772$

Probabilities from the right tail of the curve (pp. 24–25)

$Z = 0.667 \rightarrow P = 0.2527$
1 a $Z = 2.062 \rightarrow P = 0.0196$
b $Z = 1.031 \rightarrow P = 0.8487$
2 a $Z = 0.357 \rightarrow P = 0.6394$
b $Z = 1.071 \rightarrow P = 0.1421$

Probabilities on the left of the curve (p. 26)
$Z = 1.333 \rightarrow P = 0.4087$

Probabilities from the left tail of the curve (pp. 27–28)
$Z = 2 \rightarrow P = 0.0228$
1 a $Z = 2.577 \rightarrow P = 0.005$
b $Z = 1.031 \rightarrow P = 0.3487$
2 a $Z = 1.786 \rightarrow P = 0.0370$
b $Z = 0.357 \rightarrow P = 0.1394$

Probabilities from both sides of the curve (p.29)
$Z_{155} = -1 \rightarrow P = 0.3413$
$Z_{180} = 0.667 \rightarrow P = 0.2477$
Total probability = 0.5890

Probabilities from two tails of the curve (pp. 30–31)
$Z_{200} = 2 \rightarrow P = 0.0228$
$Z_{150} = 1.\dot{3} \rightarrow P = 0.0913$
Total probability = 0.1141
1 a 0.7876 (GC: 0.7877) b 0.0206
2 a 0.5027 (GC: 0.5025) b 0.6859

Calculating probabilities by difference (p. 32)
$Z_{160} = -0.667$, P = 0.2477
$Z_{162} = -0.533$, P = 0.2029
Total probability = 0.2477 – 0.2029 = 0.0448

Mixing it up (pp. 34–37)
1 a $Z = 2.273$, P = 1.15%
b $Z = 0.455$, P = 0.3508 (GC: 0.3506)
c $Z = -1.364$, P = 0.9137
d $Z = -2.273$, P = 0.0115, so 0.0115 x 130 = 1.495, so one or two kakapo.
2 a $Z = 1.429$, P = 0.0765 (GC: 0.0766)
b $Z_{9500} = -0.714$, P = 0.2624
$Z_{1100} = 1.429$, P = 0.4235
Total probability = 0.6859
c $Z_{8500} = -2.143$, P = 0.4839
$Z_{9500} = -0.714$, P = 0.2624
Total probability = 0.2215
d $Z_{8000} = -2.857$, P = 0.0022, so 0.0022 x 950 = 2.09, so about 2.
3 a $Z = 2.5$, P = 0.0062
b $Z = 1.25$, P = 0.7888 (GC: 0.7887)
c $Z = 0.625$, 73.40%
d $Z = -2.5$, P = 0.0062, so 11160 bottles could be expected to hold less than 1 L.
4 a $Z = 1$, P = 0.3413
b $Z = -1.286$, P = 0.0992 (GC: 0.0993)
c $Z_{90} = -0.571$, P = 0.2160
$Z_{110} = 0.857$, P = 0.3042
Total percentage = 52.02% (GC: 52.05%)
d $Z = 1.571$, P = 0.0581, so number of people taking longer than two hours is about 22.

2 Inverse normal calculations (pp. 38–51)

Using a probability to find Z (p. 38)
1 $Z = 2.42$ 2 $Z = 0.16$
3 $Z = 3.00–3.02$ 4 $Z = 1.005$
5 $Z = 1.965$ 6 $Z = 0.549$
7 $Z = 1.758$ 8 $Z = 2.144 – 2.146$
9 $Z = 0.109$ 10 $Z = 2.383 – 2.385$

Using Z to calculate the value of x — where Z is positive (pp. 39–40)
1 $Z = 0.841$, $x = 182.62$ cm 2 UQ = 135.5 kg
3 120 marks 4 Weights above 240.5 g

Using Z to calculate the value of x — where Z is negative (pp. 41–42)
1 $Z = -1.281$, $x = 150.79$ cm 2 Minimum weight = 100.7 kg
3 91 marks 4 Height = 47.92 cm

Using Z to calculate the mean (pp. 44–45)
1 $Z = -2.5$, $\mu = 180$ cm 2 $\mu = 55.93$ g
3 $\mu = 502$ g 4 $\mu = 100{,}021$ hairs

Using Z to calculate the standard deviation (pp. 46–47)
1 $Z = 1.2$, $\sigma = 15$ cm 2 $\sigma = 23$ kg
3 $\sigma = 56.95$ g 4 $\mu = 54\%$, $\sigma = 10.4\%$

Mixing it up (pp. 48–51)
1 a 0.45 g b 81.3%
2 a 5.8363 days or 140.1 hours
b LQ: 5.7894 days or 149.1 hours, UQ: 6.2106 days or 138.9 hours
3 a $\mu = 504$ mL b 34.5 → 35 bottles
4 a $\sigma = 15{,}600$
b Between 91,819 km and 108,180 km
5 a 163 marks b 127 marks
6 a $\mu = 209$ million litres/s
b 250 million litres/s
7 a $\sigma = 24.32$ g b Minimum weight = 190.0 g
8 a Anna because she is late 95.87% of days. Mike is late on 94.26% of days.
b Anna takes 7 minutes 59 seconds, so both must leave at 8.22 a.m.

3 Mixed normal distribution problems (pp. 52–53)

1 a P = 0.4235 (GC: 0.42343)
b P = 0.0022 (GC: 0.0021373)
c $\mu = 10{,}500$ hours
d $\sigma = 1934$ hours
e $\mu = 10{,}972$ hours
2 a P = 0.4087 (GC: 0.40878)
b P = 0.9772 (GC: 0.97724)
c 2736 (GC: 2731)
d Species B has 4.78% (Species A has 4.1%)
e Height = 27.82 m, 96.54% can be milled.

Probability trees (pp. 54–62)

pp. 56–62
1 b 0.22 c 0.135
d 0.55 e 0.355
f 568 failed g 0.67
h 0.33. This is 1 – 0.67 because all students must belong to either those in **f** or those in **g**.
2 b 0.42 c 0.24
d 0.48 e 23
f 0.7 + 0.06 = 0.76 g $\frac{P(BM)}{P(M)} = \frac{0.24}{0.28 + 0.24} = 0.4615$
h $\frac{P(WB)}{P(B)} = \frac{0.42}{0.42 + 0.06} = 0.875$
3 a 1.61% b 8.05 → about 8
c 98.39% d 23%
e 25.72%
4 a $\frac{7}{8} = 0.875$ b $\frac{3}{8} = 0.375$
c $\frac{1}{3}$
5 a $\frac{16}{216} = 0.0741$ b $\frac{10}{16} = 0.625$
6 a 0.12 b 0.32
c $\frac{0.18}{0.32} = 0.5625$
7 a $\frac{12}{380} = 0.0316$ b $\frac{248}{380} = 0.6526$
c $\frac{90}{132} = 0.6818$ d $\frac{720}{6840} = 0.1053$
e $\frac{864}{6840} = 0.1263$ f 7
g 8

ISBN: 9780170354240

8 Note: P(HF) = 0.123 → P(healthy tree is felled = 0.3)
a 0.6835 b 0.82
c 1600
9 a 0.57 b 0.6485
c 0.3986
10 a 0.27 b 0.7037
c 0.5135
11 a $\frac{358800}{6497400} = 0.05522$ b $\frac{24}{6497400} = 3.693 \times 10^{-6}$
c $\frac{96}{6497400} = 1.478 \times 10^{-5}$ d $\frac{24336}{6497400} = 0.003745$
e $\frac{28561}{6497400} = 0.004396$ f $2 \times \frac{109850}{6497400} = 0.03381$

Probability tables (pp. 63–70)

Tables of frequencies (p. 64)

a 0.092 b 0.184
c 0.5217
d Cars that are unregistered are more likely to have no warrant of fitness than those that are registered.
e 0.228 f 920
g 8878, so estimate is 9000 (also allows for spares)

Creating your own table (p. 66)

a

	Girls	Boys	Total
Sport	360	420	780
No sport	264	156	420
Total	624	576	1200

b 0.5769 c 0.4615
d 27.08% e 0.78
f 72.92% of boys play sport, but only 57.69% of girls play sport. Therefore he should target the girls.
g $\frac{0.7292}{0.5764} = 1.265$ so boys are only 26.5% more likely to play sport, not 30% more. So the headline is not justified.

Tables of probabilities (pp. 68–70)

a

	Bike	Foot	Total
Males	0.31	0.21	0.52
Females	0.14	0.34	0.48
Total	0.45	0.55	1

b 0.2917 c 0.3111
d 1300 e 897
f 62.07%
g P(male did it on foot) = 0.4038.
P(female did it on foot) = 0.7083.
$\frac{0.7083}{0.4036} = 1.754$ so his boss is not correct because 1.754 is less than 2.

1 a

	Girls	Boys	Total
Bus	25	50	75
Other	15	10	25
Total	40	60	100

b 0.625 c Three-quarters (0.75)
d More than three-quarters of boys must also arrive by bus.
e 0.9 f 84
g

	Girls	Boys	Total
Bus	148	282	430
Other	84	56	140
Total	232	338	570

2 a 0.6061 b 0.2189
c 61.28% d 0.3298
e 0.5076
f Fish eaters were about one and a half times more likely to select mussels as a starter than steak eaters.
g 0.3872
h 126.6, so estimate that he should order 130.

Risk (pp. 71–78)

Risk and tables (pp. 73–78)

1 a

	Late	On time	Total
Walk	21	9	30
Bus	11	14	25
Total	32	23	55

b 0.5818 c 0.7
d 0.44 e $\frac{0.7}{0.44} = 1.59$
f Mere is about 1.6 times as likely to be late for school if she walks rather than catches the bus.
2 a 0.222 b 0.27
c 0.15 d $\frac{0.27}{0.15} = 1.8$
e Students who drank three alcoholic drinks were 1.8 times as likely to fail the coordination test than those who drank three non-alcoholic drinks.
f 51. It would not be surprising if 53 passed the test because 60 is a relatively small number and by chance two more people than expected might pass.
3 a

	Cold	No cold	Total
Days off	0.14	0.065	0.205
No days off	0.21	0.585	0.795
Total	0.35	0.65	1

b 0.35 c 0.4
d 0.1 e 4
f Students who caught a cold were four times as likely to take days off school than those who didn't catch a cold.
g $\frac{0.2642}{0.6829} = 0.3869$
h Students who didn't take days off school were only 39% likely to catch a cold compared with those who did take time off.
4 a

	Hip fracture	No hip fracture	Total
Diabetes	12	1488	1500
No diabetes	55	8445	8500
Total	67	9933	10,000

b 0.0012 c 0.008
d 0.0065 e 1.236
f This means that for those aged 66 or older, diabetics are 20% as likely to fracture a hip than non-diabetics (or 1.2 times as likely).
g $\frac{0.1791}{0.1498} = 1.1956$
h This means that for those aged 66 or older, those with hip fractures are 20% as likely to have diabetes than those who haven't fractured a hip (or 1.2 times as likely).
5 a 0.024 b 0.09
c 3.75
d Children between the ages of three and six who consume soft drinks between meals are 3.75 times as likely to have one or more molars extracted than those who are not.

ISBN: 9780170354240

6 a 2.739×10^{-5} b 2.888×10^{-7}
c $(2.739 \times 10^{-5}) \div (2.888 \times 10^{-7}) = 94.84$

7 a Risk of having the form of cancer if you test positive $= \frac{0.000098}{0.000098 + 0.00999} = 0.0097 \approx 0.01$
b Risk of not having the form of cancer if you test negative $= \frac{0.98901}{0.98901 + 0.0000002} \approx 1$

8 20% of 5 = 1
So the absolute risk of catching the disease for those who take the drug is 0.04.

9 a 25% of 0.0004 = 0.0001
So the absolute risk of developing this form of cancer if the diet is followed is 0.0003.
b One person

Practice questions (pp. 79–84)

Practice question one (pp. 79–80)

a $\frac{8}{28} = 0.2857$

b

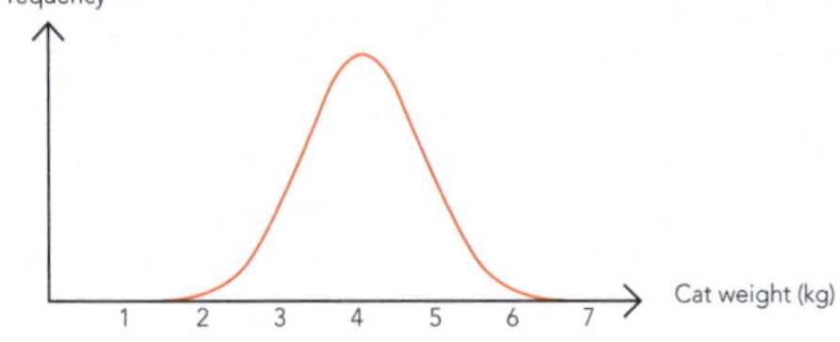

Bell-shaped, centred on 4.1 and tapering to about 1.7 and 6.5 (±3 SD).

c $Z = 1.125$ → P = 0.3696 (GC: 0.3697) ∴ 45 cats.

d $0.3696^2 = 0.1366$ (GC: 0.1367)

e $Z = 2.375$ → P = 0.0088. number of cats over 6 kg is 30.8, i.e. 31.

f UQ = 4.639 kg, LQ = 3.561 kg

g Domestic cat distribution is bimodal, with modes at 1–1.5 kg and 3.5–4 kg, whereas the distribution of feral cats is unimodal with a mean of 4.1 kg. Overall, feral cats are bigger.
The spread for weights of domestic cats is between 0.5 kg and 5 kg, a total range of 4.5 kg, but the spread for the feral cats is larger, from about 1.7 kg to 6.5 kg, a total range of about 4.8 kg.
The bimodal distribution of the domestic cat distribution is not symmetrical compared with the normal-shaped distribution of feral cats, which is symmetrical.

Practice question two (pp. 81–82)

a 0.0642

b 0.2761

c 4.3. This means that an unvaccinated student was 4.3 times as likely to catch the flu than a vaccinated student.

d Expected number of people in first school who would have had flu had they not been vaccinated
$= 327 \times 0.2761 = 90.28$
Number of vaccinated students who were prevented from getting the flu
$= 90.28 - 21 = 69.28$
Likely number of students prevented from getting the flu in larger school
$= 69.28 \times \frac{2976}{950} = 217.03$
So 217 students prevented from getting the flu.
Assumptions:
1 Same rate of uptake of vaccinations.
2 Same strains of influenza.
3 Similar physical conditions in school — ventilation, etc.

e 0.03

f $0.046 \times 95 = 4.37$ → about 4

g $\frac{0.15}{0.02} = 7.5$ This means that unvaccinated members are seven and a half times as likely to get the flu.

Practice question three (pp. 83–84)

a 0.0189

b 0.4762

c 10

d $\frac{0.01 \times 0.9}{0.99 \times 0.01} = \frac{10}{11}$

e $\frac{0.01 \times 0.9 \times 0.95}{0.99 \times 0.01 \times 0.05} = 17.27$

f $(0.00855 + 0.000495) \times 900 = 8.1405$, so about 8.

ISBN: 9780170354240